Creeds in Contrast

A Study In Calvinism and Arminianism

by
Dale M. Yocum

Schmul Publishing Co.

Schmul's Wesleyan Book Club Nicholasville, Kentucky

Published by Schmul Publishing Co.
PO Box 776
Nicholasville, KY 40340

Printed in the United States of America

ISBN 0-88019-183-X

Contents

Introduction

IS THE BIBLE REALLY true? Does it possess ultimate authority on all matters whereof it speaks? Does its message determine the content of creeds? Have the creeds sometimes had a tendency to bend the Bible to the conclusions of their logic?

To the first three questions conservative Christians would surely answer, "Yes," though to the fourth, perhaps an equivocal "No." And yet, as this book by Dr. Dale Yocum points out, there have been occasions in the history of Christendom when the philosophical bias of the major architects of some creeds has influenced their conclusions away from a balanced view of Scripture rather than in accordance with it.

The title of the book, *Creeds in Contrast*, might seem to some to be only a study of the disagreements between two schools of thought. And yet one senses this is not the ultimate intent of the author. What is really being asked, and answered, is the question, "What saith the Scripture?" Does the Bible teach unconditional predestinarian election for each individual, or does it allow for free human response to the call of the Gospel? Does the sovereignty of God determine all that occurs, or does God sometimes limit *the exercise* of His sovereignty in the interests of moral and personal integrity? Does the Bible teach that God has decreed from all eternity that only a limited number of people shall be saved? Or does it say that, "Whosoever shall call upon the name of the Lord shall be saved?" In each instance of contrast, the latter answer is shown to be the answer of Scripture.

This book deals with many questions in addition to the three cited above, and in every instance the balanced answers of Scripture are given in a most convincing manner. The fact that these answers are Wesleyan-Arminian, and not Calvinistic, is incidental to the all pervading emphasis that the Scriptures rightly interpreted are allowed to speak the final word.

To read *Creeds in Contrast* should renew to all the sense of importance of these issues. While there is much that is highly beneficial to be found in the writings of men like Augustine and others, nonetheless it is evident that sometimes philosophical presuppositions were factors in their interpretation, whether they were aware of it or not. It is to the credit of James Arminius that the conclusions of sound exegesis took precedence over the theology of John Calvin, especially in Romans seven and nine. The conclusions he reached were costly, and his aversion to controversy prompted him to put them in as inoffensive a language as possible. Even so, the differences were too great to be dismissed in cavalier fashion, as both sides understood, and so must we.

Dr. Yocum is eminently qualified to write this book. He has served in the classroom as well as the pulpit. He has been, and is, a missionary as well as an evangelist. He has a clean, burning heart for people and for what the Apostle Paul called "the truth of the Gospel" (Galatians 2:5, 14). He has searched the Scriptures for countless hours. He has demonstrated fair play with those who differ theologically, and yet his experience on the front lines of theological battle has taught him repeatedly that sound doctrine is essential for right thinking, for Christian experience and living. These distinctions do make a difference—perhaps an eternity of difference!

The conclusions reached by Dr. Yocum are clear, cogent, convincing and, I would add, *conclusive*. I heartily recommend this book to all who wish to know the truth that makes us free indeed! (John 8:32-36).

ELDON R. FUHRMAN, PH.D.
Professor of Theology
Wesley Biblical Seminary
Jackson, Mississippi

Preface

INSPIRATION FOR THE PREPARATION of this book came while the writer was occupied as an instructor in the Holiness Theological Seminary in Seoul, Korea. Awareness that many students and preachers with a rich background in Wesleyan teaching were losing that heritage by neglect caused some interested persons to request that this work be prepared. After considerable deliberation and study, it was undertaken—with the conviction that such a study is indeed vital. As I have visited other mission fields, the same need has appeared again and again. In the United States, as well, there is need for a fresh emphasis on the importance of clear and correct doctrine. Hopefully, such a treatise as this will help to meet that need.

It should be acknowledged at once that people may hold to incorrect doctrines, within limits, and still live consistent lives of godliness. I am thankful to have many very dear friends of deep piety who hold to doctrinal positions with which I take issue in this study. May such a production as this not rupture those friendships!

In spite of such considerations, it is vital to see truth as it is set forth in the Word. While it is possible for people to reach Heaven while holding some errors in doctrine, we ought, nevertheless, to avoid those doctrinal errors that are hazardous to spiritual welfare and destiny. Two of the hazards may be mentioned. First is a cheapened view of sin and salvation. Any doctrine that makes it appear safe to go on sinning while believing in Christ is hazardous in the extreme. The Bible standard for believers is holy living, not sinful living. The second danger grows out of the first. If it is possible for a believer to fall away and be lost, then a doctrine to the contrary is perilous indeed. It may bring one to the judgment with a false confidence of safety. Apparently, Jesus referred to just such an occurrence when He said, "Many will say to me in that day, Lord, Lord, have we not prophesied in thy name? and in thy name have cast out devils? and in thy name done many wonderful works? And then will I profess unto them, I never knew you: depart from me, ye that work iniquity" (Matthew 7:22-23). Here are people, many in number, who are active religiously, but who have an apparent conviction that sin will not bar them from Heaven. It is a shattering disillusionment to them that sinful living is in itself a sure barrier to entrance into the eternal kingdom of God. Their doctrinal position, whatever its justification for sinning as Christians, was tragically in error!

With such a conviction of the seriousness of the issues involved, the book has been written. May God bless its going forth, as He has blessed my own soul in the study and preparation of it!

Special thanks are due to my wife, who so faithfully worked on typing the manuscript and suggesting necessary corrections; and to Drs. Eldon R. Fuhrman and Wilbur T. Dayton, at that time president and vice president, respectively, of Wesley Biblical Seminary in Jackson, Mississippi, and to Rev. Robert Shank of Mt. Vernon, Missouri, for carefully reading the manuscript and making valuable suggestions; as well as to a number of other friends who contributed valuable counsel.

Mere change in doctrine is not the goal in view. My prayer is that through this study, some may come not only to illumination of doctrinal truth, but to a life of liberty, cleansing and power by the Spirit of Christ!

To God be all the glory!

DALE M. YOCUM

Prairie Village, KS

November, 1985

1

Historical Backgrounds

DOCTRINAL STATEMENTS ARE MADE more meaningful for us when we understand the intense debates which have been involved in the formulations of doctrine and the personalities who have engaged in those debates. This chapter is a brief review of the theological issues which have developed into the classical positions of Calvinism, on one hand, and Wesleyan-Arminianism, on the other. It includes reference to some of the outstanding men who have championed these divergent positions with mental astuteness and moral courage. Even when we may disagree with the conclusions reached by such champions, we may, nevertheless, admire their intensity and labor in promoting what they believed to be the truth.

The Scriptural Origin

Probably no part of Scripture has been more involved in the controversy concerning predestination than St. Paul's Epistle to the Romans, particularly chapters nine to eleven. Yet, interestingly, in those chapters the author was in reality seeking to correct errors similar to those which were later championed by theologians of the Calvinistic school.

In the days of St. Paul many of the Jewish leaders strongly resented the preaching of the gospel to the Gentiles. They believed that, since the Jews were God's elect, they were thus predestinated to divine favor. They could not understand how it was possible for them to be set aside while the Gospel was preached to the Gentiles. Surely God's predestination meant that they, and they only, were assured of His eternal favor. How could they ever be bypassed and the Gentiles brought into divine favor? Was that not a contradiction of God's predestination and election?

So St. Paul wrote in detail to explain the meaning of election. He endeavored to show the difference between national election, which is unconditional, and individual election, which is conditional. He explained how Israel could be set aside temporarily as a nation, and individuals among the Israelites could be lost because of unbelief, while Gentile individuals could be saved by faith and become a part of spiritual Israel. God's predestination was not violated when individual Israelites were lost and Gentiles saved or while the Jews were temporarily cut off from the living vine and the Gentiles were grafted in. When Israel shall come as a nation to faith in Christ, then as a nation it will be restored to divine favor. In the meantime, both Jews and Gentiles must come to salvation through personal faith in Christ.

A more detailed discussion of these strategic chapters will be given later. Here it is only necessary to say that they were written to counter just such misconceptions as are current among the predestinarians of today.

Augustine and the Pelagians

From the days of the Apostles until the time of Augustine (354-430 A.D.), the Church taught that Christ died for all men and that any man could be saved by responding to the invitation of the gospel. Election and predestination were viewed as conditional and corporate, applying to the body of Christ and being subject to the personal exercise of faith. Because of such belief, that early Church was intensely evangelistic, hastening to take the message of salvation to every part of the known world.

Early in the fifteenth century a British monk named Pelagius went to Rome and began to oppose the generally-accepted doctrines of human depravity and the necessity of prevenient grace to personal salvation. He taught that in Adam's sin he only injured himself and that his sin was not transmitted to the entire race of men. Every human soul has an innate capacity for good and needs only the help of instruction to attain to personal holiness. The law is as good a means to perfection as the gospel, and men with their own ability can perfectly keep the law if they desire to do so. The grace administered by the Holy Spirit is helpful, but not absolutely necessary, to the attainment of salvation.

Such a position as that of Pelagius carries to the extreme a view of the importance of human free will. He believed the will, in itself, to be capable of keeping the law and of gaining perfection.

Against such extreme views another Roman Catholic scholar, Augustine, directed his energies, for he saw a most dangerous heresy in them. Initially he had taught the freedom of the will in response to the universal call of the Gospel. God's predestination, he said, depended on His foreknowledge of those who should believe; and believing lies within the power of man. After becoming involved in the controversy with Pelagius, however, he modified his views. He then took a very strong position concerning the inherited depravity of man, calling it "original sin." Such inherited sin renders man totally incapable of any good. His will has no power whatever to seek or to find any means of salvation. It is only by the sovereign and irresistible will of God that men can be saved. God acts directly upon the will of man, turning it away from sin to receive salvation. Man thus has no power over his own will, except as a sinner; in the sinful state the will freely seeks after sin. When God acts upon a man, though, He takes control of the will and saves him. The will is no longer free.

If it were true that Christ died for all men, Augustine reasoned, then all men would be saved. If God wills the salvation of all men, and His will is irresistible, then all must necessarily be saved. It is an easily-observed fact, however, that not all men are saved. The conclusion to which Augustine was thus forced is that God does not will the salvation of all men. Instead, God evidently chooses certain men to be saved and leaves the rest helpless in their sins, awaiting judgment. This being true, it is also evident that Christ did not die for all men, but only for those who are predestined to be saved.

Augustine thus arrived at his doctrine of predestination at the end of his course of reasoning, in reaction to the extremes of the Pelagian position. He did not take it from the Scriptures but developed it as logical conclusion of his prior reasoning. This fact is worthy of notice, for very often the proponents of predestination, charmed by the logic of their theological system, have brought their conclusions to the Word of God for verification; and when there is no adequate verification in the Word, they have interpreted the Word to conform to the logical system rather than to modify the system until it conforms to the Word.[1]

Although Augustine fashioned a theology of rigid predestination, he continued to preach a gospel available to all and urged men freely to choose the way of life rather than of death. Frequently in Christian history the same has occurred: the doctrine preached has been at variance with the theology professedly believed. Men with an evangelistic spirit have not been willing to limit the gospel appeal in a way which a strict application of their theology would dictate. This very fact has caused many men to turn away from such a doctrine.

Calvin and His Creed

One of these consequences of the Protestant Reformation was a new appeal to the word of God by laymen. Luther had insisted that the humblest layman had a right, under the guidance of God, to interpret the Scriptures and to apply them to his own life. The result of this new sense of freedom was an increase of confusion in the minds of many people. The average layman was not sufficiently informed in the Word of God to make sound interpretations.

Into this confusion came John Calvin (1509-1564), a brilliant man expertly trained in theology, law and the Holy Scriptures. Initially he was a Roman Catholic, and his purpose was to help to reform the church from within. The intensity of persecution which came upon him, however, persuaded him that such a course was impossible. So he left the church and began a ministry of teaching and writing, which was in large measure influenced by conditions within the Catholic Church.

Some of the strong emphases of Calvin were the authority and sufficiency of the Scriptures, the Presbyterian form of church government, separation of Church and State, and the necessity of personal piety.[2] Certainly the teaching for which he has become most famous, though, is that of predestination. It was advanced partly as a means of repudiating the Catholic doctrine of good works and merit.

Although Calvin was logical in his thinking, he did not carry all of his reasoning to its logical conclusions. His followers enlarged and increased the precision of the theological system which he developed and presented in his treatise, *Institutes of the Christian Religion*, first published in 1536.

As an example, Calvin taught double predestination; that is, the predestination of some to eternal life and of others to eternal damnation.

> By predestination we mean the eternal decree of God, by which he determined with himself whatever he wished to happen with regard to every man. All are not created on equal terms, but some are preordained to eternal life, others to eternal damnation; and, accordingly, as each has been created for one or the other of these ends, we say that he has been predestinated to life or to death.[3]

However, Calvin was reluctant to go so far as to make God the author of sin. He labored earnestly to free his doctrine from such a conclusion, but involved himself in some inconsistency in doing so. In his book *Concerning the Eternal Predestination of God* (10:7) he said,

> It must be observed that the will of God is the cause of all things that happen in the world; and yet God is not the author of evil...Whatever things are done wrongly and unjustly by man, these very things are right and just works of God.

A little later, in paragraph 11, Calvin supported Augustine's words:

> Who does not tremble at these judgments with which God works in the hearts of even the wicked whatever he will, rewarding them none the less according to desert?...God works in the hearts of men to incline their wills just as He will, whether to good for His mercy's sake or to evil according to their merits.[4]

The inconsistency between those two is evident: in the first Calvin said God is not the author of evil; in the second he said God works in the hearts of men, inclining them either to good or to evil.

Calvin's successor at the university which he established in Geneva, Switzerland, was Theodore Beza (1519-1605). Beza was less inhibited than Calvin was and boldly declared that God in His absolute predestination causes men to sin. He did not originate the idea; he simply stated it as a conclusion which he felt was inevitable from the logical premises of Augustine and Calvin.

The followers of Calvin summarized his teaching in terms of the famous "five points," as follows:

1) Total depravity, by which men are naturally unable to do anything toward their own salvation.

2) Unconditional election, or particular predestination, by which each person is divinely chosen either for eternal life or eternal damnation.

3) Limited atonement, providing for the salvation only of those who are elected to eternal life.

4) Irresistible grace or effectual calling, by which it is absolutely assured that those who are elected shall be saved.

5) Final perseverance, or unconditional security, by which it is assured that those who once savingly believe on Christ shall be eternally preserved from falling away.[5]

Within one generation the doctrines of "Calvinism" spread across the continent of Europe and to the British Isles. This fact was largely due to the influence of the *Institutes*, which were published often in new and enlarged editions; and to the University of Geneva, where Calvin and Beza had a growing influence. It opened in 1559 with 162 students and increased to over 1,600 students by 1565. Trained religious leaders went forth to spread the doctrines they had learned all over Europe.

Arminius and the Remonstrants

The progress of Calvinism in the Netherlands was complicated by a difficult political situation. The country was under the dominion of a Spanish monarch, and Protestants were severely persecuted by the Roman Catholics, who were in alliance with the political authority. The Calvinists, although at first in the minority, became leaders in a growing revolt against the rulers, whom they considered to be tyrants. They had an ally in the person of Prince William of Orange, who held it as his duty to protect the interests of the people against tyranny of all kinds. After 1585 the northern provinces of the country were essentially free from Catholic domination, and Calvinism began to flourish.

About this time there appeared a brilliant scholar, James Arminius (1560-1609), whose teaching, preaching, and writing were strongly to challenge the Calvinistic theology and greatly influence the subsequent course of Christian thought. He came from a poor home, and his father died while he was still young. His talent was recognized by others, though, and leaders of the state church in Amsterdam provided him an education at the University of Geneva, with the understanding that he would come to be their pastor if they should call him.

At Geneva Arminius studied under Beza and was thus indoctrinated in the tenets of the highest form of Calvinism. Upon returning to Amsterdam he soon established a reputation for fervent preaching and able exposition of the Word of God.

In 1589 a well-educated layman named Koornheert arose to oppose the theological position of Beza. He insisted that if God causes sin, as Beza said, then God is in reality the author of sin. The Bible, he said, does not teach such a serious error as this. His brilliant argument was attracting increasing crowds of people, who were being strongly influenced by his teaching. It was such a serious threat to the Calvinistic theology, and to the government, since the church and state were associated at this time, that Arminius was commissioned to study and refute the teachings of Koornheert. In response to the request, he gave himself to a diligent study of the scriptural teaching about predestination, particularly in Romans, chapters nine to eleven. The more deeply he searched into the meaning of St. Paul, the more clearly he saw that, while they support general predestination, according to which God is shown to be ultimately sovereign over men and nations, they do not teach the kind of predestination Beza was expounding. To the contrary: although Israel was raised up as a nation by the election of God, individuals of that nation must personally appropriate salvation by faith. The nation for a time was cut off because of the unbelief of her people, and Gentiles became a part of "spiritual Israel" by faith.[6]

Probing farther in his study, Arminius discovered that none of the early church fathers had held to such a view of predestination as Beza espoused. Instead they had consistently presented the gospel freely to all, with the conviction that any person who freely responded in faith could be saved.

Now thoroughly convinced that the Calvinistic tenets were erroneous, Arminius began to teach what he believed to be the truth about the issues of predestination, election and the atonement. He did not do this in a sensational way, for he disliked controversy. He felt obligated, though, to stand with the truth of God against the errors of men.

In 1575 Prince William of Orange ordered the establishment of a university in Leyden, and in 1602 Arminius was appointed as a member of the theological faculty. Here he came into conflict with Gomarus, professor of New Testament at the university. Gomarus held to the entire system of high Calvinism and insisted that Arminius should do the same. He declared that the Holy Scriptures must be interpreted according to the Calvinistic creed, while Arminius insisted with equal vigor that the Bible, not the Calvinistic creed, was the final authority.

Arminius showed with logical clarity that if the Calvinistic system were carried to its proper conclusion, then God would indeed be made the source of all sin in the universe, just as Koornheert had said. So effective was he in presenting the scriptural support for his position that nobody could prove him in error. His calm logic, deep piety, and forceful use of scriptures made it impossible for anybody to stand effectively against him.

His adversaries were not to be silenced, however. They began a whispering campaign against him, spreading the view that he was a heretic and seriously perverting his position. This deeply pained Arminius, who greatly cherished unity in the Body of Christ and did not want to be involved in a conflict of personalities. He sought to have a council arranged where the issues could be discussed and decided, without a fracture in the fellowship of the church. Such a forum was denied, though, until after his death. In the meantime, he continued to write extensively concerning the truths which are revealed in the Word of God.

The followers of Arminius, who became known as "Remonstrants" because of their opposition to Calvinism, prepared a summary of their position in contrast to the "five points" of Calvinism. These became known as the "Remonstrant Articles." They may be summarized as follows:

1) God decreed that in Christ He would bestow salvation on those who, as He foresaw, would believe on Jesus Christ and persevere in their faith unto the end.

He would inflict everlasting punishment upon those who would persist in unbelief unto the end.

2) Jesus Christ by His suffering and death made an atonement for every man, but only those who believe on Him shall be partakers of the salvation thus provided.

3) Because man is depraved in nature, he has no power in his own will to save himself. Therefore he must receive the grace of God before he can believe and be saved.

4) Everything that may be called good in man comes by the grace of God. This grace does not force man to act against his own inclination, but may be resisted and finally rejected.

5)Those who are united to Christ as believers may receive an abundance of grace and strength to withstand all of the temptations which they may encounter. By neglecting such grace and strength, though, they may fall from grace and finally perish.[7]

After Arminius' death, the political and ecclesiastical powers arranged for a council to be held to debate and decide the theological issues. The Synod of Dort (1618-1619) was thus convened, but it was an entirely one-sided affair. The Arminians were brought in as prisoners in chains and were not allowed to speak in behalf of their views. The decision was consequently in total support of the Calvinistic position, which was precisely formulated in terms of the five points of Calvinism.

We must remember that the decision was political as well as theological, so we cannot condemn the doctrinal position just because the political authority went to such extreme in banning all Arminian pastors from their pulpits, imprisoning Hugo Grotius, one of the leading Remonstrants, for life, and even beheading Barnfeldt, one of the Arminians. It is an illustration of the grievous ills which can occur when the church is united with political power.

Arminius died before the Synod of Dort. His influence did not die, though, for with the harsh repression in the Netherlands, Arminian pastors went to other countries preaching the doctrine they so strongly believed.

Wesley and Wesleyanism

In England Calvinism penetrated the established Church of England until it became quite Calvinistic in its theology. One of the young men who grew up in this church was John Wesley (1703-1791). Early in his life he had a great desire for spiritual perfection, that he might serve God with all his desire and strength. He hoped to gain such perfection through strict discipline and good works, and so he was not fully satisfied during the years prior to his true conversion. That came in 1738, and from that time he began to preach justification by faith alone without the aid of good works. Because of such an emphasis, he was increasingly barred from the established church, which held that good works were necessary to salvation. So he began to preach to large crowds in the open air and gained many converts. These were gathered into religious societies for spiritual counsel and growth, but were not at first organized into a separate denomination. It was only when the societies began to be planted in America that the Methodist Church was officially organized.

In his declaration of justification by grace through faith, Wesley was very close to the Calvinist position. He differed from Calvinism in several important regards, however, and in much the same way as Arminius did. Wesley was much impressed with the work of Arminius and for a time edited a magazine entitled the "Arminian." He summarized the differences between the two positions in terms of three contrasts: 1) The Calvinists hold to absolute predestination, while Arminians hold to conditional predestination. The condition refers to receiving and believing the Word of God. 2) The Calvinists hold that grace is absolutely irresistible, whereas the Arminians believe a person may resist that grace and be lost. 3) The Calvinists hold that a true believer never can fall from grace and be lost. Arminians believe that they can.[8]

In one very important regard, Wesley went beyond the doctrine of Arminius; he held a higher view of sanctification. He believed that through the power of the Spirit a person could be fully sanctified by faith as definitely as he could be justified by faith. Through much of his life and ministry he proclaimed the message of perfect love, or "Christian perfection." The Methodist Church was raised up to proclaim this message, and for many years it did so with great effectiveness.

Part of the challenge for Wesley's strong emphasis on holiness was because of the antinomianism of his day. As a result of strong Calvinistic teachings (among the Moravians, for example), it was commonly believed that since salvation is by grace alone and not by any works of men, it is therefore not necessary for men to obey the law of God in order to be children of God. In fact, it was sometimes said that since God is glorified in the forgiveness of sins, the more a person sins the more glory he brings to God! Wesley strongly took issue with such dangerous teaching and with the interpretations of Calvinism which gave support to it. A close associate of Wesley, John Fletcher, wrote his famous *Checks to Antinomianism* as a refutation of the Calvinistic positions which tend toward a light regard of sin in the lives of the believers. The teaching of Wesley and Fletcher was a strong call for holy living and a declaration that the energizing fullness of the Spirit makes holy living possible!

The combination of Arminianism and Wesleyanism was a strong influence in the promotion of evangelism and missionary activity. The doctrine of Calvin—in particular, the emphasis on election and predestination—was stifling to evangelistic passion. If by the sovereign decree of God and His irresistible grace, certain ones were predestined to be saved and others were equally certain of perdition, then there was no real urgency for missionary zeal and evangelistic activity. The Arminian emphasis on the universal call of the gospel and the necessity of offering salvation to all men and nations introduced a new impetus for evangelism. The Wesleyan message not only carried forward the same emphasis; it added the dynamic of a cleansed life and the empowering fullness of the Holy Spirit as enablement for the work of evangelism. A mighty renewal came into missionary activity. Not only in the British Isles, but across the ocean to America and into other nations, went impassioned messengers of full salvation. They carried not only a message of salvation from sin but of compassion on the needy in every stratum of society. It has been shown by John Wesley Bready in his book *This Freedom: Whence?* that through the Wesleyan influence there came an end to slavery in the British Empire and in America as well.[9] Much of the evangelistic thrust in America, Asia, and other parts of the world today can be traced back to Wesleyan-Arminian beginnings, as we shall see.

Neo-Calvinism

Early in the seventeenth century certain Christian leaders of France, such as Camero and La Place, began to modify the Calvinistic idea of a limited atonement. They held that Christ truly died for all men, but that none are morally able to respond to the call unless God sovereignly applies His grace to them. Because men do have the natural ability of choice, however, they held that men are responsible for their rejection of the atonement. They still retained the idea of election, because God has chosen those whom He will enable morally to respond to His call.

Because of the influence of Arminius and Wesley, there came further deviations from strict Calvinistic doctrine. In New England (North America), there arose what were called the New Social Calvinists, including such men as Jonathan Edwards, Timothy Dwight, and Charles G. Finney. These men did not agree exactly in all points, and Finney even came quite close to the Wesleyan position. They departed progressively from the doctrine of a rigid, particular predestination.

Under the preaching of Jonathan Edwards (1703-1758), the first great revival, called "The Great Awakening," came to America. Another revival followed in the next century, with Charles Finney as the outstanding evangelist. Of the spreading spirit of revival, John H. Bratt, writing from a strong Calvinistic viewpoint, says,

> The major revivals after the Great Awakening were designed to reclaim the thousands who had pushed across the frontier in the Westward trek and had failed to keep their church membership vital...The denominations most active in frontier evangelism were the Methodists, the Baptists, and the Presbyterian Reactionaries, all of whom were impelled by an Arminian theology...
>
> The later revivals led by Moody and Billy Sunday went in the same direction, so that Arminians became firmly entrenched and evangelism in America today is predominantly Arminian in theology.[10]

What Bratt calls Arminianism is in reality a modified or mild form of Calvinism, influenced greatly by the Arminian theology. The precise theological position varies from one group to another, but in general there is emphasis on a universal atonement, a sincere gospel appeal to all men to receive Christ by faith for personal salvation, and acceptance of the unconditional eternal security of believers.

Summarizing the present condition in America, Bratt says,

> Calvinism in America today is a 'struggling remnant.' There are, to be sure, individual Calvinists and groups of Calvinists in the evangelical denominations, but organizationally, there are only five or six denominations that are still quite thoroughly imbued with Calvinism.[11]

He then proceeds to list the Christian Reformed Church, Orthodox Presbyterian Church, Reformed Presbyterian Church, Associate Reformed Presbyterian Church, Evangelical Presbyterian Church, Reformed Church in the United States, Protestant Reformed Church, Bible Presbyterian Church, and the Free Christian Reformed Church.

In the foregoing list it is noteworthy that there are no Baptist churches listed. They would generally be classed as mildly Calvinistic or thoroughly Arminian.

Writing concerning Baptists, Dr. William J. Adams, former professor in the Southern Baptist Theological Seminary, says,

> Let it be remembered that, less than a hundred years ago, all five cardinal points of Calvin's system of theology generally prevailed among Baptists, as theological textbooks of the times will confirm. Today, only one point remains to any appreciable extent among Baptists, inevitable perseverance, and there is growing evidence that Baptists are increasingly questioning this last vestige of the central core of Calvin's system of theology.[12]

The Wesleyan-Arminian churches today are primarily the holiness groups, such as the Church of the Nazarene, Wesleyan Church, Free Methodist Church, and a number of other smaller denominations. Some individual Methodist churches are in this category also, although the denomination as a whole has been very liberalized.

The Situation in Korea

(*Note*: The following section was written for the Korean edition of this book. It is of sufficient historical interest, however, that the publisher suggests its inclusion in the English edition. Those not interested in the holiness movement of Korea may skip this section without affecting in any way their understanding of subsequent portions of the book.)

Although Methodist and Presbyterian missionaries came to Korea as early as 1885, the Wesleyan emphasis on holiness did not begin until early in the present century. Charles E. Cowman had established a Bible institute in Tokyo, Japan, and three Korean students were sent back to open a mission in Seoul. From the very beginning the special blessing of God was upon the work.

> On Sabbath afternoons when Christians gathered at the meeting for promotion of Scriptural Holiness, numbers sought and obtained the blessing, returning to their own churches veritable flames of fire.[13]

After the opening of a Bible training institute in Seoul, growth continued in a marvelous way:

> The story of the transformation of whole regions through the power of the Gospel, carried on by men of faith, constitutes a thrilling record. Up to the year 1927, fifty-seven churches had sprung up and scores of itinerant points, while about half of Korea has been visited by Korea Village Campaign Bands, resulting in hundreds, yea, thousands of earnest seekers. The seekers in villages during 1927 numbered 5,564.[14]

As Charles Cowman observed these wonderful miracles of salvation through the power of the Holy Spirit, he recognized that it was not the work of men alone, but God answering the prayers of many people. Looking ahead, he said with prophetic insight, "Unless we maintain our standards, the whole work goes down."[15]

What were the standards which he held so tenaciously? As a genuine evangelical, he believed strongly in the inspiration and authority of the Scriptures, regeneration by the Holy Spirit, divine healing and the second coming of Christ. But the distinctive doctrine, which gave the movement its early name in Korea, was that of scriptural holiness.

> He never disguised his view of sanctification, and was often heard to remark, "I believe it right up to the hilt, that the Blood of Jesus Christ His Son cleanseth me from all sin." He did not believe that a child of God could *grow* into sanctification any more than a sinner could *grow* into a saint. He believed and taught that a "born again" soul came to a place, if he walked in the light, when he would as truly cross over into the promised land as did Joshua when he set up a heap of stones as a witness of the crisis step taken. He never deviated one jot from that standard.[16]

That was the standard which Charles Cowman knew must be maintained. There is a crisis of entire sanctification which a believer enters by faith, when his heart is purified by the blood of Jesus Christ. It was to that crisis experience that those early believers witnessed as they returned to their own church "veritable flames of fire."

> His convictions on the subject of heart holiness were grounded upon a close study of the Word, and he never failed to let his belief in the blessed experience be well understood, often in circles where it cost something to be firm and true.
>
> He was never known to compromise the truth for the sake of prestige. He did not forget the purpose of his journey, nor his life that had been committed to the sacred trust. He never sold the truth to save the hour. There is too much compromising and trimming in this our day; the age needs men of stern fidelity to God and His cause.[17]

Unfortunately, not all of those who have adopted the name of holiness in Korea have held as strongly to the doctrine and experience as that saintly founder did. It is a matter of history that in about 1945, as Korea was released from Japanese occupation, certain holiness leaders reasoned that in order to achieve the maximum growth, there should be decreased emphasis on the distinctives of holiness truth. Increasingly the form of worship was patterned after that of the Presbyterian Church, which had achieved greater growth. Ministers stocked their bookshelves with Calvinistic books. The call to a definite experience of holiness was heard less and less. Clear testimony to cleansing from sin, such as Charles Cowman so courageously maintained, was almost altogether silenced.

When certain of the churches associated with the largely-Calvinistic International Council of Christian Churches, the invasion of Calvinistic doctrines increased. Presbyterian ministers came to pastor holiness churches and to teach in holiness schools, without leaving their Calvinistic beliefs behind. Motivated by common interests, they rejoiced in the fellowship thus made possible. But the decay of the Wesleyan message was progressing.

One man who had been an officer in a holiness seminary for thirteen years told the writer that during all of that time, he had not known the difference between a holiness church and a Presbyterian church. Many students coming forth from the seminaries were in the same position. It is not rare to find students from what are still called holiness churches who have never heard one clear message on the crisis experience of heart cleansing through the blood of Christ or a single, vibrant testimony to such an experience. They do not know the difference between Wesleyanism and Calvinism.

These lines are not written with any desire to disrupt fellowship between Christian brethren, but rather to declare the necessity of a wonderful heritage that rightfully belongs to the Holiness Church of Korea.

Charles Cowman said, "Unless we maintain our standards, the whole work goes down." Numerically the work still advances, but that fact can never alleviate the loss when people are no longer cleansed from sin, filled with the Holy Spirit, and sent forth as flaming evangelists of transforming truth! In one year of village evangelism—in 1927—there were more than 5,500 people won for Christ. Today there are still many thousands of villages in South Korea that need the Gospel of Christ! It is time for a renewal of the Wesleyan message! It is time for a revival of holiness in doctrine, in experience, and in holy living!

Endnotes

1. Illustrations will be given in appropriate places later.
2. John H. Bratt, ed., *The Rise and Development of Calvinism* (Grand Rapids, MI: Wm. B. Eerdmans Publishing Co., 1959), pp. 29-32.
3. John Calvin, *Institutes of the Christian Religion*, Book III, Chap. xxi, Para. 5. (Hereafter references to the *Institutes* will be given in the form III:xxi:5.)
4. John Calvin, *Concerning the Eternal Predestination of God* (London: James Clarke and Co. Limited, 1961), pp. 169, 177.
5. See Bratt, *Op. cit.*, p. 84.
6. A detailed analysis of Romans 9 to 11 is given in Chapter 8.
7. H. Orton Wiley, *Christian Theology* (Kansas City, MO: Beacon Hill Press, 1952), Vol. II, p. 351.

8. *The Works of John Wesley*, authorized edition published by The Wesleyan Conference, London, 1872 (14 vols; photo offset edition; Kansas City: Nazarene Publishing House, 1958), Vol. X, pp. 359-60; hereafter referred to in the form Wesley, *Works*, X, pp. 359-60.

9. John Wesley Bready, *This Freedom—Whence?* (New York: American Tract Society, 1942).

10. Bratt, *Op. cit.*, pp. 125-26.

11. *Ibid.*, p. 133.

12. Robert Shank, *Life in the Son* (Springfield, MO: Westcott Publishers, 1961), p., 16. (The Introduction was written by Dr. Adams.)

13. Lettie B. Cowman, *Charles E. Cowman, Missionary Warrior* (Los Angeles: The Oriental Missionary Society, 1943), p. 206.

14. *Ibid.*, p. 213.

15. *Ibid.*, p. 210.

16. *Ibid.*, pp. 237-38.

17. *Ibid.*, pp. 238-39.

2

The Sovereignty of God

THE TERM "SOVEREIGNTY" REFERS to the supreme authority of government invested in a person or group. It involves freedom from limitation by any external power or authority. No term that could be properly translated "sovereign" occurs in the Old Testament. The Greek word *pantokrator* is variously translated as "almighty," "omnipotent," or "sovereign" in different translations. It occurs ten times in the New Testament, nine of them in The Revelation.[1] Each time the word refers to God as the supreme power in the universe.

Every person who believes the Bible will surely agree that God is sovereign in the world which He has created—that He is never forced into any action by any external power, contrary to His own will and purpose. While accepting this common tenet, though, various groups do differ strongly concerning some of the implications of God's sovereignty. In this chapter we will study some of the serious differences in Calvinistic and Arminian schools of thought.

The Calvinistic Position

Its Derivation

Augustine was the first of the church fathers to formulate a doctrine of absolute sovereignty of God in such a way as to deny the possibility of man's will opposing God's will. In a basic handbook of the Christian faith entitled *Enchiridion* he wrote of God the Father, "For he is called Almighty for no other reason than that he can do whatsoever he wills, and because the efficacy of his omnipotent will is not impeded by the will of any creature."[2]

Since this interpretation of God's irresistible sovereignty is the foundation for all the Calvinistic system, it is important to note that it was not derived from the Scriptures, but from philosophical considerations. Then the Scripture was interpreted in such a way as to make it conform to the basic tenet of the system.

As one example among numerous ones that could be cited, we may observe Augustine's treatment of 1 Timothy 2:4. He said,

> When we hear and read in sacred Scripture that God "willeth that all men should be saved," although we know well enough that not all men are saved, we are not on that account to underrate the fully omnipotent will of God. Rather, we must understand the Scripture, "Who will have all men to be saved," as meaning that no man is saved unless God wills his salvation: not that there is no man whose salvation he doth not will, but that no one is saved unless He willeth it."[3]

The passage from St. Paul directly contradicts Augustine's basic tenet; but to protect his system, Augustine reinterpreted St. Paul to make him say something consistent with that system. Thus, instead of conforming his doctrine to the Scripture, he forced Scripture to conform to his doctrine. By such a method a man can support any doctrine he may choose to believe.

John Calvin adopted and enlarged the teaching of Augustine, upholding the claim that no other will can resist God's will. In his *Institutes* he said,

> Now, since the arrangement of all things is in the hand of God, since to him belongs the disposal of life and death, he arranges all things by his sovereign counsel, in such a way that individuals are born, who are doomed from the womb to certain death, and are to glorify him by their destruction...Since he foresees the things which are to happen, simply because he has decreed that they are to happen, it is vain to debate about prescience, while it is clear that all events take place by his sovereign appointment.[4]

Like his predecessor, Calvin also took great liberties in interpreting God's Word. Concerning the passage, "God will have all men to be saved," he wrote, "By this he assuredly means nothing more than that the way of salvation was not shut against any order of men... Since it clearly appears that he is speaking not of individuals, but of orders of men, let us have done with a longer discussion."[5]

St. Paul's words plainly speak of all men and God's will that they all be saved. But since this contradicts the basic assumption of his system, Calvin reinterpreted Paul's words to mean something else, that God only purposes to save some of all classes of men, while reserving the rest to damnation. It is of interest that Calvin disagreed with Augustine in interpreting the passage; but both of them forced the passage to fit their theological presuppositions. If such liberties of interpretation are to be accepted, then it is impossible ever to establish a consistent biblical theology. Any interpreter can make the Bible mean whatever he wants it to.

A more recent writer, who seeks to apply the Calvinistic system with logical consistency, has put the case for God's absolute sovereignty thus:

> The sovereignty of the God of Scripture is absolute, irreversible, infinite...We affirm that He is under no rule or law outside of His own will and nature, that God is a law unto Himself, and that He is under no obligation to give an account of His matters to any...His power is exercised *as* He wills, *when* He wills, *where* He wills...For a long season, that power appears to be dormant, and then it is put forth in irresistible might.[6]

In elaborating his position Pink asserted that God has determined in Himself from all eternity everything that will be and that no other power can withstand His will.

The Problem of Human Freedom

Two vital questions arise as a consequence of such a rigid view of the sovereignty of God. What measure of freedom is there in the human will? And who is responsible for sin in the world? These questions merit extensive consideration; but since they arise again in connection with predestination (Chapter 3), they will be treated more thoroughly there.

Augustine held that no human will can hinder the divine will from its complete fulfillment. God wills those who shall be saved and those who shall be condemned eternally. But because Augustine did not want to attribute to God the responsibility for men's sins, he found himself in a very difficult position from which he could not satisfactorily extricate himself. The awkwardness of his effort is evident in the following quotation:

> For as far as related to themselves, these sinful creatures did what God wished not to be done; but in view of God's omnipotence, they could in no wise effect their purpose. For in the very fact that they acted in opposition to his will, his will concerning them was fulfilled. And hence it is said that "the works of the Lord are great, well considered in all his acts of will." For it would not be done did he not permit it (and, of course, his permission is not unwilling, but willing).[7]

That is indeed an "unspeakably strange and wonderful" kind of action in which what is done in opposition to God's will is nevertheless the fulfillment of His will, because He is omnipotent! It is further evidence of how reason as well as Scripture was bent to conform to Augustine's philosophical system of thought.

Calvin, in his efforts to honor the sovereignty of God and yet give proper place to the human will, involved himself likewise in several obvious contradictions. He agreed with Augustine that man was originally free, but that through the fall he came under the bondage of necessity. Approvingly, he quoted Augustine thus: "Man through liberty became a sinner but corruption, ensuing as the penalty, has converted liberty into necessity." Then he continued with his own evaluation, seeking to preserve human freedom,

> Man, since he was corrupted by the fall, sins not forced or unwilling, but voluntarily, by a most froward bias of the mind; not by violent compulsion, or external force, but by the movement of his own passion; and yet such is the depravity of his nature that he cannot move except in the direction of evil. If this is true, the thing not obscurely expressed is, that he is under a necessity of sinning.[8]

Note the contradiction: first Calvin asserted that men are not forced or unwilling in their sins; then he followed by saying they are under necessity—they cannot move in any direction but evil.

We may observe a few more of the contradictions into which Calvin fell. Describing the original condition of man, he said, "In this upright state, man possessed freedom of will, by which, if he chose, he was able to obtain eternal life...Adam, therefore, might have stood if he chose, since it was only by his own will that he fell."[9] Yet concerning the fall of Adam, Calvin wrote, "God not only foresaw the fall of the first man, and in him the ruin of his posterity; but also at his own pleasure arranged it. For as it belongs to his wisdom to foreknow all future events, so it belongs to his power to rule and govern them by his hand."[10] Now if God predestined the fall of Adam, as Calvin elsewhere stated, and if it is impossible for man to oppose the will of God which is manifested in His predestination, then it was certainly not possible for Adam to have chosen otherwise. Yet he says that Adam might have stood if he had chosen to do so. A contradiction is evident.

Another contradiction arose in his efforts to affix ultimate responsibility for the condemnation of sinful men. In defining predestination, Calvin said, "We mean the eternal decree of God, by which he determined with himself whatever he wished to happen with regard to every man. All are not created on equal terms, but some are preordained to eternal life, others to eternal damnation."[11] Notice Calvin's phrase, "with himself," which means that God made His decision without reference to anything outside Himself, as Calvin's writings amply show. Yet, in seeking to avoid any suggestion that God is responsible for sin, he called it preposterous to suggest that the origin of human condemnation is in the hidden recesses of the divine counsel, whereas the true source is in the corruption of man's nature.[12] Surely the true source of condemnation is either in God or in man; it cannot be in both. Yet Calvin ascribed it to both.

One more contradiction may be mentioned with reference to the force of immediate causes. Is it possible, as some have believed, that Adam was the immediate cause of his own fall and that God simply permitted the sinful act without thus being responsible for it? The above statement, that the true source of man's condemnation lies in his own nature, indicates that Calvin did at times assign responsibility to such immediate or secondary causes. However, in other places he rejected such an idea. He asserted that what God permits, He truly wills: there is no difference between his directive and permissive will. Even in this matter, though, he seemed to give an opposite conclusion, for he said, "While in [God] the will is one and undivided, to us it appears manifold, because, from the feebleness of our intellect, we cannot comprehend how, though after a different manner, he wills and wills not the very same thing."[13] It is indeed a serious problem if God appears to will the sins of men and at the same time wills them not, condemning forever those who commit them. Yet it is into such a position that Calvin brings us by his reasoning.

The Problem of Responsibility for Sin

Concerning the question of the ultimate responsibility for sin, Calvin sought earnestly to avoid the conclusion that God is the cause. It was this effort, out of respect for the love and justice of God, which got him into so many logical difficulties. He held that God ordained all things that are and yet that He is not the author of sin. Numerous of his followers, though, have with much less reluctance assigned to God the responsibility of ordaining sin's entrance into the world. Theodore Beza, Calvin's successor at Geneva University, pressed the theological system of Calvin to its ultimate conclusion and insisted that God causes men to sin just as truly as He causes some to be saved and some to be reprobated. Extreme Calvinism, which included this tenet, was soon spread abroad as orthodox theology, and many church leaders accepted it. Indeed, it was because of this very tenet that Arminius eventually arose to champion an opposing position.

In recent times, also, advocates of a strict Calvinism have argued forcefully for the view that God ordains all sin in the world. As an instance, we may take the position of Arthur Pink, who taught and wrote early in this century. Like Beza, he carried the teachings of Augustine and Calvin to their logical conclusion. We will consider three statements from his writing:

> To affirm that God decreed the entrance of sin into His universe, and that He foreordained all its fruits and activities, is to say that which, at first, may shock

> the reader; but reflection should show that it is far more shocking to insist that sin has invaded His dominions *against* His will, and that its exercise is outside His jurisdiction: for in such a case where would be His omnipotency?[14]

> Plainly it was God's *will* that sin *should* enter this world, otherwise it *would not* have entered, for nothing happens save as God has eternally decreed. Moreover, there was more than a bare *permission*, for God only permits that which He has purposed.[15]

> God has not created *sinful* creatures in order to destroy them, for God is not to be charged with the sin of His creatures. The responsibility and criminality is man's.[16]

In the first quotation it will be observed that the ground of Pink's "shocking" assertion is not any declaration of Scripture, but the omnipotency of God. As has been earlier observed, this is typical of the Calvinistic system: it springs from philosophical considerations rather than from scriptural ones. It is asserted that all the fruits and activities of sin have been foreordained of God.

The second excerpt declares that God's relation to sin is not that of a mere permission, but of an eternal decree and purpose. We have seen in an earlier quotation from Pink that he held the sovereign will of God to be irresistible in its power. He asserted, "To say that God is sovereign is to declare that He is the Almighty, the Possessor of all power in heaven and earth, so that none can defeat His counsels, thwart His purpose, or resist His will."[17]

In spite of such bold declarations, Pink endeavored to relieve God of responsibility for man's sins. "The responsibility and criminality is man's," he wrote.

Now responsibility, by definition, includes the ability to choose between right and wrong courses of action and to fulfill one's obligations accordingly. It is therefore contradictory for Pink to say that man is responsible for his sins when God has decreed by His irresistible purpose that man shall sin. If God has made the choice and decree that man shall sin, and if He withholds from man the ability to refrain from sinning, then God is obviously responsible for sin.

Pink is typical of many Calvinistic writers who do not want to accept the inevitable conclusion of their own logical system. He defined the sovereignty of God as absolute, and said,

> God foreordains everything that comes to pass. His sovereign rule extends throughout the entire Universe and is over every creature...God initiates all things, regulates all things, and all things are working unto His eternal glory...'According to the purpose of Him who worketh all things after the counsel of His own will.'[18]

Once a person adopts such an absolute view of the sovereignty of God, he is bound to the conclusion that out from God flows all sin as well as all holiness. Every evil thought, imagination and purpose in the universe has come from God, and He is ultimately responsible. But such writers do not want to accept that conclusion. They have too much respect for God to attribute all vileness to Him, so they labor assiduously to free Him from the conclusion of their system. When a critic points out this implication against God's character, Calvinists typically retreat into the shelter of Romans 9:20, "Nay but, O man, who art thou that repliest against God? Shall the thing formed say to him that formed it, Why hast thou made me thus?" So let it be clearly stated that when we find this fatal defect in the Calvinist system, we are not replying against God. We are rather objecting to the distorted view of God which is the logically-necessary conclusion of their doctrine. If they do not like the conclusion, they should be willing to go back and examine again the validity of their basic premise concerning the absolute sovereignty of God.

The Wesleyan-Arminian Position

James Arminius, as shown in Chapter 1, studied Calvinism of the highest type under Theodore Beza at Geneva University. It was during an intensive study of Scripture and church history that he came to question and then oppose certain elements of Calvinistic theology. A study of his writings reveals the careful logic with which he proceeded in his refutation of those errors which he discovered.

The Decrees

Arminius gave much attention to the decrees of God which had been given prominence in the teachings of Beza. Beza, who boldly asserted that God was the cause of human sin, supported Calvin in holding that God's decree of election, by which some were ordained to be saved and others to be reprobated, preceded the decrees concerning the creation and the fall of man. Arminius objected strongly to this, as it held God responsible for causing the fall into sin in order that He might reprobate those who were not elected to salvation.

A second position was held by Thomas Aquinas and his followers. Not wanting to make God responsible for all sin, they ordered God's decrees so that the decree of election followed after the decree of creation and the fall. Man was created in a natural position in which he was personally responsible if he sinned and fell. To some persons, then, God provided supernatural grace which brought salvation. Others He passed by and left in a sinful state, that they might be reprobated. But the fault was their own. Arminius rejected this position also, for he did not believe man was created in a merely natural state, but a supernatural one, in which he bore the very image of God and was supplied with grace sufficient for his needs. He reasoned also that a decree to save some was in effect a decree that men should sin, since without sin there could be no salvation.

A third position was held by Augustine and those who followed him. According to it, God first decreed to create men, then to allow the fall, then to elect some through salvation to eternal life, while others were left in their sins to merit eternal punishment. To this also Arminius objected, for he could not accept the idea that God had prepared punishment for any man from eternity without a way of salvation for them.

After a careful evaluation of the various levels of Calvinism, then, he rejected them all. His own position concerning the decrees of God was as follows: first, the decree to appoint Jesus Christ as the Mediator and Savior, to provide salvation from sin through His own death; second, the decree to save those who should repent and believe in Christ and persevere in their faith, but to leave in sin those who would not so repent and believe, finally damning them as aliens from Christ; third, to decree sufficient means, as determined by His own wisdom, whereby sinful men might be enabled to repent and believe in Christ; fourth, the decree whereby those individuals foreknown as persevering in faith were predestined to eternal life, and those foreknown as not continuing in faith were predestined to eternal punishment.[19]

Wesleyans do not generally place so much emphasis on the decrees as Arminius did, since the Scripture does not give any order of decrees whatever.

The Divine and Human Wills

In his treatment of divine sovereignty, Arminius determined to avoid making God the author of sin and to preserve the liberty of the human will. The will of God is two-fold, he stated. There is absolute will, by which He wills those things that have no relation to the will of His creatures. Then there is a relative will, by which He wills certain things with respect to the will of His creatures. In the latter category is the divine permission by which God allows a rational creature to do what He forbids or to omit what He commands. Yet in spite of this divine permission, His absolute will is powerful enough that He can bring certain ends to pass in spite of the possible opposition of His creatures. To this theme, we shall return shortly.

John Wesley supported the view of Arminius relative to the sovereignty of God. The Calvinistic position, he said, gave emphasis to God's power at the expense of His justice.

> The sovereignty of God is then never to be brought to supersede his justice. And this is the present objection against unconditional reprobation;…it flatly contradicts, indeed utterly overthrows, the Scripture account of the justice of God…How shall God in justice judge the world, if there be any decree of reprobation? On this supposition, what should those on the left hand be condemned for? For their having done evil? They could not help it. There never was a time when they could have helped it…You suppose him to send them into eternal fire, for not escaping from sin! that is, in plain terms, for not having that grace which God decreed they should never have! O strange justice! What a picture you draw of the Judge of all the earth![20]

God acts as both creator and governor in the world, Wesley asserted. As creator He has acted from His sovereign will, without counsel from any other, creating what, and when, and where He chose. He made man in His own image, giving him the power of understanding and will. As governor, God no longer acts as sovereign, but as a judge. But all judgment must pre-suppose free agency in the moral realm. Any creature without the power of choice, such as the sun or moon, is not accountable for judgment.

> Every punishment supposes the offender might have avoided the offense for which he is punished: otherwise, to punish him would be palpably unjust, and inconsistent with the character of God our Governor.
>
> Let then these two ideas of God the Creator, the sovereign Creator, and God the Governor, the just Governor, be always kept apart. Let us distinguish them from each other, with the utmost care. So shall we give God the full glory of His sovereign grace, without impeaching his inviolable justice.[21]

Frequently those writing from a Calvinistic position have questioned how God could still be sovereign if He allowed any human will to resist His own. For example, Pentecost has written,

> A widely-held interpretation is that God has elected those who He knows will accept Christ as personal Savior. This is an erroneous interpretation,…God is no longer a sovereign God if He elects those who He knew would accept Him as Savior, those who would put faith in His Son, the Lord Jesus Christ. God is then subject to the whims of the human will.[22]

This is a fair question, and it deserves a satisfactory answer: how can God allow man to exercise free choice and still maintain his own sovereignty? Let it be understood, first, that the freedom which God has granted to man is not absolute, but is set within limits which God Himself has decided—limits which are both moral and historical in nature. Morally, God has set the rules which His creatures are to obey and has "appointed a day, in the which he will judge the world in righteousness by that man whom he hath ordained" (Acts 17:31). Historically, God has determined that certain events will occur in spite of all the activities of men and devils. Nothing shall avail to prevent the consummation of history which He has ordained.

This pattern of God's sovereign rule was manifested right in the Garden of Eden. In fact, it was expressed in connection with His purpose to create the first man. "And God said, Let us make man in our image, after our likeness: and let them have dominion over the fish of the sea, and over the fowl of the air, and over all cattle, and over all the earth, and over every creeping thing that creepeth on the earth" (Genesis 1:26). Now the term "dominion" involves the right to make and enforce decisions upon those who are placed under that dominion: in this case, all other creatures in the earth. Since God assigned to Adam a realm of rule and authority, it is evident that He limited His own immediate authority. God, as ultimate governor over all, gave to Adam some instructions concerning his use of created things. He could freely eat of all the trees in the garden except one. If he should eat of that, he must die. So God's sovereignty was manifested in assigning to man his realm of rule under God's authority, in giving the rules under which Adam must act and in declaring the penalty which must be suffered if that rule were violated. In carrying out such a plan, God did in no way violate His sovereignty, for all things were done in accordance with His own planning. He foresaw the possibility of disobedience and arranged penalty accordingly. He obviously preferred that possibility to the mechanical carrying out of His own detailed rules by a creature that had no freedom.

Arminius discussed at length this problem of the will of God and the sin of man. He stated that God expressed a preceptive will and a permissive will. By His precept, He revealed what His creature of understanding and free will ought to do. By permission, He allowed the creature to violate the divine precept. His preceptive will was not issued with absolute authority and power, for that would have violated the will of the creature in an area where he was given dominion. Yet it was supported with sufficient means—a precept, a threat, and a sufficient supply of grace—whereby obedience was made possible.

> God, indeed, foresaw sin, but He did not will it; indeed, He endeavored to prevent

> it by precept and the bestowment of grace, necessary and sufficient for the avoidance of sin. Farther than this, He must not prevent, lest He should destroy the constitution which He had established.[23]

The willful sin of man, therefore, did no violence to the sovereignty of God, for God in His sovereign will had assigned to man an area where he should have the right of choice, even against the preceptive will of God.

God's Sovereign Limits

The limits which God has placed on the freedom of His creatures apply to the devil, to men, and to nations. He has permitted *the devil* to operate down through history, but within defined limits. Satan himself acknowledged such limits when he asked permission to take away Job's possessions from him and later to take even his health away. "Hast not thou made an hedge about him?" Satan asked (Job 1:10). And God has such a hedge about every one of His children, which can not be penetrated without His permission. He has assured us that He will not permit us to be overcome with temptation, which surely would occur if God didn't set such limits. "There hath no temptation taken you but such as is common to man: but God is faithful, who will with the temptation also make a way to escape, that ye may be able to bear it" (1 Corinthians 10:13).

Limits are placed upon the actions of *individuals*. They are permitted to sin if they choose, but God is able to step in and stop a course of sin whenever He chooses. Moreover, he assures the individual that every sin will be brought into judgment. "Rejoice, O young man, in thy youth; and let thy heart cheer thee in the days of thy youth, and walk in the ways of thine heart, and in the sight of thine eyes: but know thou, that for all these things God will bring thee into judgement" (Ecclesiastes 11:9).

A climactic example of limits placed upon individuals is seen in the prophecy of Daniel. He is speaking about the coming days of the Antichrist when he says,

> And some of them of understanding shall fall, to try them, and to purge, and to make them white, even to the time of the end: because it is yet for a time appointed. And the king shall do according to his [own] will; and he shall exalt himself, and magnify himself above every god, and shall speak marvelous things against the God of gods, and shall prosper till the indignation be accomplished: for that that is determined shall be done" (Daniel 11:35-36).

Please notice two of God's appointments or limits in the above quotation. There is first an appointed time, when trials and indignations shall come to the end. Second, there is a determined end of Antichrist's freedom of action. Until then, he may carry out his own will. Then he shall be certainly brought to destruction and God's people shall be delivered.

God has established certain limits concerning His dealings with *nations* as well as individuals, particularly the nation of Israel. By an unbreakable covenant with Abraham, He promised that his seed should endure forever and that they should inherit the land of promise. He has permitted to individual Israelites their freedom of action, but in spite of this fact has assured that the nation shall endure. Consider the threat of their destruction while they were in captivity. Under the edict contrived by Haman they were sentenced to be destroyed. The threat was in direct conflict with God's covenant promise. Mordecai evidently grasped the significance of this fact when he directed the following message to Queen Esther: "If thou altogether holdest thy peace at this time, then shall there enlargement and deliverance arise to the Jews from another place; but thou and thy father's house shall be destroyed: and who knowest whether thou art come to the kingdom for such a time as this?" (Esther 4:14). Mordecai recognized that, according to God's covenant, Israel must survive. Esther's role in the deliverance lay within the area where she had free choice. If she did not choose to sacrifice and participate in the effort, God would provide deliverance otherwise. He evidently did not believe the sovereignty of God foreordained the detailed actions of every person.

It is appropriate to ask at this point, does God ever change His purpose because of the contrary actions of men? According to strict Calvinists this could never happen, for it would violate the sovereignty of God. Pink wrote, "To affirm that God changes His purpose is either to impugn His goodness or to deny His eternal wisdom."[24]

Mordecai apparently believed it was God's purpose to use Esther in the deliverance, and it turned out so to be. But he also believed that if she did not respond to the challenge, God would purpose another manner of deliverance.

There are frequent examples of how God's immediate, though not His ultimate, purpose was altered in connection with Israel. When they refused to go into Canaan at Kadesh Barnea, He changed His purpose for them and declared they must wander in the wilderness for forty years (Numbers 14:34). The lesson God taught Jeremiah at the potter's house (Jeremiah 18:1-12) was that just as the potter could take a spoiled vessel and make a second-best vessel out of clay, so would God do if Israel repented. He would repent of His plan for them and do them good. But if they did not repent, He would devise evil against them.

One further example may suffice to illustrate the point. Benhadad, king of Syria, was purposed for death by the Lord, as we read in 1 Kings 20:42. God intended that Ahab, king of Israel, should put him to death when he had a good opportunity to do so. Ahab was weak in purpose and let the king go free, however. So God sent a prophet to him, saying, "Because thou hast let go out of thy hand a man whom I appointed to utter destruction, therefore thy life shall go for his life, and thy people for his people." Although God's purpose for Ahab was thwarted, His own purpose for Benhadad was accomplished, nevertheless. His death was brought about by the act of Hazael, who succeeded him as king of Syria (2 Kings 8:15). Thus can God's ultimate purposes be accomplished, although His immediate plans may be thwarted. Surely God's wisdom and power are magnified more in His ability to bring His own ends to pass in spite of the free actions of men than if He managed every detail of men and nature as robots in a mechanical fashion.

God's purposes are nowhere more vividly displayed than in relation to *Jesus Christ* His Son. From eternity, it was purposed that He should eventually be made King of kings and Lord of lords over all the earth. Yet the Father allowed men and devils to have their free opportunities, within limits, to tempt, oppose, hinder, deride, accuse, defame, condemn and crucify Him. But He came forth from the grave with such a triumph as to turn the shame into glory, death into life, and apparent defeat into climactic victory for Himself and a multitude of His followers. In a coming day, the world will arise to oppose Him again in an even more strategic show of opposition. It is plainly declared in at least nine different prophecies of the Word. One account will suffice here:

> Why do the heathen rage, and the people imagine a vain thing? The kings of the earth set themselves, and the rulers take counsel together, against the Lord, and against his anointed, saying, Let us break their bands asunder, and cast away their cords from us. He that sitteth in the heavens shall laugh: the Lord shall have them in derision. Then shall he speak unto them in his wrath, and vex them in his sore displeasure. Yet have I set my king upon my holy hill of Zion. I will declare the decree: the Lord hath said unto me, Thou art my Son; this day have I begotten thee...Thou shalt break them with a rod of iron; thou shalt dash them in pieces like a potter's vessel. Be wise now therefore, O ye kings: be instructed, ye judges of the earth... Kiss the Son, lest he be angry, and ye perish from the way, when his wrath is kindled but a little. Blessed are all they that put their trust in him" (Psalm 2).

These individual kings are not compelled to work against Christ. Instead, they are called to repentance and assured that they will be blessed if they put their trust in him. But if they unite with the majority and determine to war against Him, it is already decreed by the Father that the Son shall sit as ruler on His throne in Zion, nevertheless.

These several examples, with many others that might be given, show that God sets limits, and within them allows men and nations to exercise their freedom of choice. Because He is ultimately sovereign, however, they will not be able to prevent His final purposes from being perfectly fulfilled. Nor will they be able to escape His righteous judgments for disobeying His commands.

The Greek word often used to express God's determined will is *horizo*. Its meaning is "to mark out the boundaries or limits." The word "predestinate" is *prooridzo*, meaning to mark out limits in advance.

It is interesting that even so strong a Calvinist writer as Pink approves the idea of limits within which men and devils are permitted to work their own wills. He says,

> Christ is sovereign, supreme over all creatures. He bridles both men and demons, saying to them, as He does to the proud waves of the sea, "Hitherto shalt thou come, but no further." As the King of Zion, Christ has His chain about the necks of Satan and all his wicked instruments; and when they have gone their appointed lengths, they are obliged to stop. We see this in the case of Job: when the devil was permitted to harass him, he went only so far as his chain allowed. So it is now.[25]

It is inconsistent, however, to make such an allowance and then to insist that God is as absolutely sovereign within the limits of that chain where He *permits* rebellion and disobedience, as He is outside that limitation. For in that case, the chain means nothing whatever, and God is merely play-acting. If the chain really means something, as we insist, then God has restricted His own control within the limits of the chain in a way which does not apply outside that limitation.

The Position of the Fathers

Through his study Arminius discovered that none of the early church fathers held to a view of divine predestination which denied the free will of men in their response to the gospel call. Some statements from those fathers are included here to illustrate their position. Justin Martyr wrote in the second century A.D.,

> Lest some suppose...that we say that whatever happens, happens by a fatal necessity, because it is foretold as known beforehand, this too we explain...If...all things happen by fate, neither is anything at all in our own power. For if it be fated that this man, e.g., be good, and this other evil, neither is the former meritorious

> nor the latter to be blamed. And again, unless the human race have the power of avoiding evil and choosing good by free choice, they are not accountable for their actions of whatever kind they be. But...it is by free choice they both walk uprightly and stumble.[26]

Irenaeus of Gaul (about 130-200 A.D.) was a disciple of Polycarp, who was in turn a disciple of John the Beloved. In his work *Against Heresies*, he wrote,

> God made man a free (agent) from the beginning, possessing his own power, even as he does his own soul, to obey the behests of God voluntarily, and not by compulsion of God...And in man, as well as in angels, He has placed the power of choice,... so that those who had yielded obedience might justly possess what is good, given indeed of God, but preserved by themselves.[27]

Athenagoras, the converted Greek philosopher, wrote in his *Plea for the Christians* (about 177 A.D.),

> Just as with men, who have freedom of choice as to both virtue and vice (for you would not either honor the good or punish the bad, unless vice and virtue were in their own power; and some are diligent in the matters entrusted to them by you, and others faithless), so is it among the angels.[28]

From the *Fragments of Clement of Alexandria* (about 150-215 A.D.) comes the following assertion:

> For it is not those that abstain from wickedness from compulsion, but those that abstain from choice, that God crowns. It is impossible for a man to be steadily good except by his own choice. For he that is made good by compulsion of another is not good; for he is not what he is by his own choice. For it is the freedom of each one that makes true goodness and reveals real wickedness.[29]

Origen, the renowned theologian of Alexandria (about 185-254 A.D.), wrote in the preface to *De Principiis*,

> This also is clearly defined in the teaching of the Church, that every rational soul is possessed of free-will and volition;... we are not forced... by any necessity either to act rightly or wrongly.[30]

Chrysostom of Constantinople (347-407 A.D.) was a contemporary of Augustine (354-430 A.D.). In his *Homilies on Hebrews*, he wrote,

> All indeed depends on God, but not so that our free will is hindered. "If then it depend on God," (says one), "why does He blame us?" On this account, I said, "so that our free will is not hindered. It depends then on us, and on Him. For we must first choose the good; and then He leads us to His own. He does not anticipate our choice, lest our free-will should be outraged. But when we have chosen, then great is the assistance He brings to us.[31]

Many more examples could be cited, but this is sufficient to demonstrate the consistent position of the early fathers, which was contrary to that espoused by Augustine and the Calvinists.

A Modified Calvinistic Position

Within the last century there has been a marked swing away from the implications of strict Calvinism, particularly as it interprets the sovereignty of God. A fascinating and forthright summary of this alteration of thought has been written and well documented by Samuel Fisk. He quotes a large number of renowned men from Presbyterian and Baptist churches, and even some from the Reformed Church in America, who have abandoned the traditional Calvinistic position.

The reasons for the change of position are primarily three: rigid Calvinism is seen to be inconsistent with a proper understanding of the entire Word of God; it distorts the character of God; and it stifles both evangelism and missionary activity.

Some of the writers quoted see an apparent conflict within the Word of God which it is impossible for the human mind to reconcile. Others, by considering the self limitations of God in His sovereign actions, are able to avoid the conflict.

Considering the distortion of God's character which strict Calvinism produces, Fisk approvingly quotes Dr. A. C. Gaebelein, for many years editor of "Our Hope" magazine. Answering a question about Pink's book, *The Sovereignty of God*, Gaebelein said, "It presents God as a Being of injustice and maligns His holy character. The book denies that our blessed Lord died for the ungodly. According to Pink's perversions, He died for the elect only."[32]

Summarizing the effect on evangelism, Fisk states,

> No wonder missionary leaders are deeply concerned by the fact that Wesleyan and Pentecostal groups in Latin America are increasing at an astonishingly greater rate than our more staid and conventional groups. They at least (in spite of points on which we cannot concur with them), go out after their fellow men as if each and every one could and should respond to the gospel. It has been observed that they show a concern and a tenderness and a sense of urgency lacking in those who are assured that all is already fixed and determined in the plan of God.[33]

The foregoing paragraph refers to some points of disagreement with Arminian groups. It should be made clear that the group of men quoted have not entirely abandoned the Calvinistic position. Generally, they still find fault with Arminianism. But a careful investigation will show that what they reject is a false view of Arminianism. They understand the Arminian view of human free will as being essentially one of salvation by works. For example, Bishop Christopher Wordsworth, once Canon of Westminster and author of more than 75 published works, while taking a modified position with regard to Calvinism, nevertheless charges Arminianism with error. He says,

> They who abuse free will and reject what [God] offers, and what He desires them to accept, shall fail of salvation, and incur punishment and perdition... But in making this statement, we must not fall into the Arminian error, which represents man's goodness, foreseen by God, as the ground of God's predestination of the godly.[34]

This charge of error to Arminius is a misrepresentation of his teaching, as is shown by his comment on Romans 8:29, "For whom he did foreknow he also did predestinate to be conformed to the image of his Son, that he might be the firstborn among many brethren." Arminius stated, "He is not in error who says that *foreknowledge or prescience of faith in Christ* is signified in Romans 8:29, unless he adds the assertion that the faith, referred to, results from our own strength and is not produced by the free gift of God."[35] By this statement Arminius declares—what is consistent with all of his teaching—faith is not a work performed in human strength, for which the believer receives merit. It is rather the result of prevenient grace from God, which enables faith to be exercised in the atoning work of Christ.

It would appear that those who have rejected the extremes of Calvinism need to give more careful attention to the teaching of Arminius. They are much nearer to his position than to that of Calvin!

Endnotes

1. 2 Corinthians 6:18; Revelation 1:8; 11:17; 15:3; 16:7, 14; 19:6, 15; 21:22.
2. Augustine, *Confessions and Enchiridion*. Vol. VII of *The Library of Christian Classics* (Philadelphia: The Westminster Press, 1955), p. 395.
3. *Ibid.*, p. 401.
4. *Institutes*, III:xxiii:6.
5. *Ibid.*, IIIxxiv:16.
6. Arthur W. Pink, *The Sovereignty of God* (Grand Rapids, MI: Baker Book House, 1930), pp. 25, 26.
7. Augustine, *Op. cit.*, p. 399.
8. *Institutes*, II:iii:5.
9. *Ibid.*, I:xiv:8.
10. *Ibid.*, III:xxiii:7.
11. *Ibid.*, III:xxi:5.
12. *Ibid.*, III:xxiii:9.
13. *Ibid.*, I:18:3.

14. Pink, *Op. cit.*, p. 308.

15. *Ibid.*, p. 182.

16. *Ibid.*, p. 123.

17. *Ibid.*, p. 23.

18. *Ibid.*, p. 293.

19. *The Writings of Arminius*, Trans. by James Nichols and W. R. Bagnall (Grand Rapids, MI: Baker Book House, 1956), Vol. I, pp. 247-48.

20. *Works*, X, p. 221.

21. *Ibid.*, X, p. 363.

22. J. Dwight Pentecost, *Things Which Become Sound Doctrine* (Grand Rapids, MI: Zondervan Publishing House, 1965), p. 139.

23. Arminius, *Op. cit.*, Vol. III, p. 308.

24. Pink, *Op. cit.*, p. 207.

25. Arthur W. Pink, *The Divine Covenants* (Grand Rapids, MI: Baker Book House, 1973), p. 232.

26. Alexander Roberts and James Donaldson, editors, *The Ante-Nicene Fathers* (Grand Rapids, MI: Wm. B. Eerdmans Publishing Co., 1972 reprint), Vol. I., p. 177.

27. *Ibid.*, Vol. I, p. 518.

28. *Ibid.*, Vol. II, p. 142.

29. *Ibid.*, Vol. II, p. 581.

30. *Ibid.*, Vol. IV, p. 240.

31. Philip Schaff, editor, *The Nicene and Post-Nicene Fathers* (Grand Rapids, MI: Wm. B. Eerdmans Publishing Co., 1969 reprint), Vol. XIV, p. 425.

32. Quoted in Samuel Fisk, *Divine Sovereignty and Human Freedom* (Neptune, NJ: Loizeaux Brothers, 1973), p. 24.

33. *Ibid.*, p. 87.

34. Quoted in *Ibid.*, p. 73.

35. Arminius, *Op. cit.*, Vol. III, p. 315.

3

Divine Foreknowledge and Predestination

THE ONE TERM WHICH perhaps more than any other identifies the Calvinistic doctrine in the mind of the average person is the term *predestination.* While there are other differences between that doctrine and Arminianism that are just as significant, it is true that the differences in interpretation of predestination and foreknowledge are real and significant. We will view the Calvinistic position first.

The Calvinistic Position

Although in our chapter heading foreknowledge precedes predestination, it is logically necessary to reverse the order in considering the Calvinistic understanding, for according to that view, foreknowledge follows after predestination. Calvin said, "[God] foresees the things which are to happen, simply because he has decreed that they are so to happen."[1] Thus God first decreed, or predetermined, events, and in consequence thereof, He foreknows that what He has decreed will surely happen.

Predestination Defined

Calvin gave his definition as follows: "By predestination we mean the eternal decree of God, by which he determined with himself whatever he wished to happen with regard to every man. All are not created on equal terms, but some are preordained to eternal life, others to eternal damnation."[2] From the definition it appears that predestination relates to the destinies of volitional creatures, whereas the sovereign ordination of God applies to all events whatever, as was seen in the last chapter.

The decrees of God are the expressions of His predestination, especially as they relate to the salvation or damnation of mankind. Calvin took a strong position, which was reinforced and advocated by his successor, Beza, saying that before the creation it was decreed there should be a fall into sin involving the entire race. But even before either the decree concerning creation or the fall, there were the decrees concerning election and reprobation. Some were chosen to enjoy eternal life and others to suffer eternal damnation. Such election was made without reference to anything foreseen in the individuals, either good or bad, but simply as an expression of God's sovereign right to do anything He chose concerning His creatures and to magnify His justice.

Implications

We must now observe some implications of such a theological position. They have already been introduced (Chapter 2), but logically require further treatment here. First, it is implied that *all sin has occurred by the decree of God.* Calvin expressed it thus: "God not only foresaw the fall of the first man, and in him the ruin of his posterity; but also at his own pleasure arranged it."[3] He tried to avoid making God the author of sin, as we observed in Chapter 2. "Man therefore falls, divine providence so ordaining, but he falls by his own fault."[4] Because God has willed it, it is necessary, for all that God wills is thus made necessary. Even so, the fault was man's, Calvin insisted. It was this inconsistency which Arminius so strongly rejected, a matter to be further explained later.

A second implication of God's predestination is *the eternal damnation of non-elect infants.*

> I again ask how it is that the fall of Adam involves so many nations with their infant children in eternal death without remedy, unless it so seemed meet to God? Here the most loquacious tongues must be dumb. The decree, I admit, is dreadful; and yet it is impossible to deny that God foreknew what the end of man was to be before he made him, and foreknew, because he had so ordained by his decree.[5]

The reasoning behind the belief that infants may be elected to damnation is expressed in the Westminster Catechism. It states,

> 1. Our first parents being seduced by the subtilty and temptation of Satan, sinned in eating the forbidden fruit. This their sin God was pleased, according to his wise and holy counsel, to permit, having purposed to order it to his own glory...
>
> 3. They being the root of all mankind, the guilt of this sin was imputed, and the same death in sin and corrupted nature conveyed to all their posterity, descending from them by ordinary generation.[6]

Note, according to the Confession, that Adam's sin has been imputed to all his descendants, including infants, so that in Adam all of his posterity acquired guilt equal to his. Consequently, infants merit eternal death even before they reach the age of accountability. Such a decree Calvin admitted is dreadful, but since God foreknew it would occur, and since His foreknowledge follows from His predestination, it is a necessary consequence of His predestination as Calvin understood it.

A further serious implication of Calvin's position concerns *the freedom of men.* He and his followers insisted that men are free, but their definition of freedom differs from that of Arminian theologians. Whatever is voluntary is free, Calvin said, then proceeded to explain that the volitions of sinful men are bound by a complete necessity to continue in sin. Adam was free to choose either good or evil. When he chose evil, depravity so affected the entire race that every person's will is totally bound to sin. Until touched and changed by grace, each person is free only to sin, not to refrain from sinning. But because sin follows from his own will, he is free in his sinning and thus is personally responsible for his sin.

A recent writer for the Reformed position, Dr. John Gerstner of the Pittsburgh Theological Seminary, has said,

> If God predestinates the actions of free agents and free agents operate in such a way that they choose what seems good to them, then manifestly in predestinating the actions of free agents God has taken the choices of men for granted. And in some profoundly mysterious way what God decrees is what seems good to man... God's predestination of every act of men is the same thing as pre-determination of the freedom of men. That is, it is the acts of free agents which are predestined![7]

In further discussion, Dr. Gerstner makes more clear what that "profoundly mysterious way" is in which God acts to predetermine the conduct of His creatures. Since, according to him, men always do what they most want to do, then God, in order to determine what men shall do, simply predetermines what they shall want to do! In acting according to the desire which God has predetermined within him, the person is free because he does what he desires to do. So God's predestination confirms the freedom of the individual, for he does what he himself desires to do, although both the desire and the act are predetermined by God Himself.

A standard dictionary definition of the word *free* includes two concepts: 1) not under the control of any person or power beyond one's own nature; and 2) done voluntarily and at one's own pleasure. Calvinists such as Gerstner exclude the first meaning and apply only the second in their use of the word. Such use of the term is not only a violation of proper definition; it is a violation of scriptural usage as well. Three passages may be cited in evidence.

Jesus said, "Whosoever committeth sin is the servant of sin" (John 8:34). It may be granted that the one who commits sin does so "voluntarily and at his own pleasure." Calvinists of Gerstner's position say that such sinners are under God's control since He bestows the desire upon them. But Jesus said those sinners are under the control of sin—they are its servants. It cannot be both ways unless the Calvinists equate God with sin.

Similar reasoning applies to Paul's words in Romans 6:16, "Know ye not, that to whom ye yield yourselves servants to obey, his servants ye are to whom ye obey; whether of sin unto death, or of obedience unto righteousness." It is impossible to yield oneself unto sin—of one's own volition—without being a servant of sin. Again, the contradiction of Gerstner's position is shown.

Finally, Romans 7:16-17 exhibits the opposite condition, in which a sinner desires not to sin but is under a control beyond his own desire. "If then I do that which I would not,... it is no more I that do it, but sin that dwelleth in me." The control beyond immediate desire, Paul says, is sin; the Calvinists say it is God. Again, God must be equated with sin to justify their position. This is precisely the charge which Arminius made against their doctrine.

A theology which must violate both common word meanings and scriptural statements to support a doubtful doctrine is not acceptable.

Foreknowledge Defined

We come now to a consideration of foreknowledge. Calvin said,

> When we attribute prescience [foreknowledge] to God, we mean that all things always were, and ever continue, under his eye; that to his knowledge there is no past or future, but all things are present,... He truly sees and contemplates them as actually under his immediate inspection. This prescience extends to the whole circuit of the world, and to all creatures.[8]

Thus God's foreknowledge means that He knows all things, past, present and future with equal clarity as if they were all present.

Implications

Foreknowledge, for Calvinists, involves the absolute certainty of the actions foreknown. "If foreknowledge be true, the absolute certainty of all the actions of free agents is certain from all eternity; because, if they were not certain then God could not foreknow them as such."[9] Along with predestination, then, it serves to assure that every event is foreordained from all eternity.

As was mentioned at the beginning of this chapter, predestination precedes foreknowledge in the mind of God. Pentecost gives a typical explanation:

> Foreknowledge, as used in Scripture, refers to what God knows with certainty will come to pass because He has decreed that event… Foreknowledge, then, is the result of God's foreordination, or God's decree, of what will take place… Foreknowledge says nothing of what God knew the individual would do, but foreknowledge has to do with what He would do with men.[10]

The reason why Calvinists are so insistent on this order is because to reverse it would in their estimation violate the absolute sovereignty of God. If God's decrees were in any measure modified by what He foreknew man would do, in believing or refusing the gospel, then His sovereign power would be responsive to the actions of men. According to their definition of sovereignty, that would be a contradiction. If God should respond to the will of men, then He would no more be sovereign. To be sovereign He must determine or foreordain the responses of men to the gospel. He knows the response in advance because He has decreed it in advance.

To summarize, God's predestination means that from all eternity He has determined, simply from His own sovereign will, every event whatever, but particularly concerning human salvation or damnation. His foreknowledge arises from His predestination. He knows what will occur because He has decreed it shall. Some Calvinists assert that God's knowledge even includes a disposition toward or against the persons known, so that His foreknowledge as well as His predestination is determinative of what He will do concerning every individual.

The Wesleyan-Arminian Position

Dr. Wiley has observed that the Arminian position concerning predestination and foreknowledge did not originate with Arminius and, therefore, should rather be called the catholic (universal) position. It was held from the days of the apostles to the time of the Reformation and characterized the teaching of Lutheran and Anglican theologians, as well as those of the Greek and Roman Catholic Churches.[11] Of course it has also been held by those who adopt the interpretations of Arminius. One example may illustrate this claim of antiquity. Origen wrote against the views of Celsus early in the third century A.D.,

> Celsus imagines that an event, predicted through foreknowledge, comes to pass because it is predicted; but we do not grant this, maintaining that he who foretold

> it was not the cause of its happening, because he foretold it would happen; but the future event itself, which would have taken place though not predicted, afforded the occasion to him, who was endowed with foreknowledge, of foretelling its occurrence.[12]

Foreknowledge and Human Freedom

Arminians generally believe in the omniscience of God, that is, His perfect knowledge of all things, past, present and future. Arminius allowed this, but made a distinction in the modes of God's knowledge. He does not know the contingent actions of His creatures in exactly the same way as those which proceed simply from Himself. By nature, knowledge of the actions of free creatures proceeds from those actions. That is, the knowledge comes from the action, and not vice versa. [13]

The renowned theologian Richard Watson explained the Arminian position in detail. Free, or contingent, actions may be certain actions, but they cannot be necessary actions and still be free, he said.

> The certainty of a *free* action does not result from the knowledge of it, which is no cause at all, but from the voluntary cause, that is, the determination of the will. It alters not the case in the least, to say that the voluntary action might have been otherwise. Had it been otherwise, the knowledge of it would have been otherwise; but as the will, which gives birth to the action, is not dependent upon the previous knowledge of God, but the knowledge of the action upon the foresight of the choice of the will, neither the will nor the act is controlled by the knowledge; and the action, though foreseen, is still free or contingent.[14]

Admittedly, the relation between foreknowledge and freedom is difficult for us to comprehend, since we have always lived within a time frame. God is not so bound to time, as He "inhabiteth eternity" (Isaiah 57:15). Our certain knowledge that the sun shone yesterday is in no way the cause of its shining. Similarly, although God knows certainly what the choices of free individuals will be, the knowledge does not cause, and thus does not make necessary, those free actions.

To make the matter more clear, it may be noted that God's foreknowledge of the future is not a simple knowledge of what shall be, but a perfectly complete knowledge of all possible alternatives, if His free creatures had made other choices. One among many examples from the Bible is found in 1 Samuel 23. David and his men had gone to the walled city of Keilah and saved it from the Philistines. Saul heard of the event and determined to capture his enemy there.

Upon inquiring of the Lord about this purpose of Saul, David was told that Saul would indeed come to Keilah and that the men of the city would deliver David into his hand. Here is the Bible record: "Then said David, Will the men of Keilah deliver me and my men into the hand of Saul? And the Lord said, They will deliver thee up. Then David and his men, which were about six hundred, arose and departed out of Keilah, and went whithersoever they could go. And it was told Saul that David was escaped from Keilah; and he forebare to go forth" (vv. 12-13). God's statement concerning what was going to happen was plainly conditioned upon the actions of David. If he stayed in Keilah, he would be delivered into the hand of King Saul. But he did not remain there; so he was not delivered into his hand. God's statement of the future was based on His certain knowledge of alternative courses of action. What He knew did not actually come to pass, because it involved the voluntary response of a man, and that man chose not to remain in Keilah.

Wesley agreed with Arminius that the perfect foreknowledge of God is no cause of events whatever. He added a further emphasis that, strictly speaking, there is no such thing as either knowledge or afterknowledge with God. All of time and eternity are immediately known to Him so that He does not see one thing as before another. They are not necessary because He knows them, however; rather, He knows them because they occur. To his treatment of freedom we shall return later.

Arminius' "Declaration of Sentiments"

Arminius opposed the concept of unconditional predestination with forceful logic. In his "Declaration of Sentiments," he gave twenty reasons for rejecting the doctrine. Space permits mention of only a few of them.[15]

1. The doctrine of predestination is no part of the gospel, for the gospel contains a call to repentance and faith, which is followed by a promise of eternal life. But predestination contains neither the call nor the promise. Men are predestinated unconditionally, without reference to anything they will ever do or be. The doctrine does not tell us what kind of men are predestinated, because God's decrees of election and reprobation were made without reference to God's foresight of whether or not men would believe on Jesus for their salvation. There is no hint in the doctrine as to why God chose certain ones and rejected others. But the gospel declares that those who repent and believe shall be saved. Therefore predestination is no part of the gospel.

2. None of the respected teachers of the church and none of the church councils, for the first 600 years of the Christian era, admitted or approved such a doctrine of predestination as the Calvinistic system recommends.

3. The doctrine is contrary to the justice of God, for it affirms that He has willed to save certain men and to consign others to eternal perdition without any reference whatever to any righteousness done or sin committed by the individuals involved. Since predestination is settled entirely apart from divine foreknowledge of character, the destiny is determined arbitrarily, independent of moral conduct. This is entirely repugnant to God's justice.

4. The doctrine is contrary to the goodness of God, for it states that He, influenced by nothing outside Himself, willed the greatest conceivable evil to some of His creatures and did so from all eternity, before He resolved to bestow any portion of good upon them. He first willed to damn them eternally, and then willed to create them in order that He could damn them. This is entirely contrary to the biblical concept of God's goodness.

5. The doctrine essentially changes the nature of sin; for, according to scriptural teaching, sin is the meritorious cause of damnation. This doctrine, though, makes sin merely the means by which God carries out His predetermined reprobation. The doctrine thus changes sin from a cause to a mere means, and these two are manifestly different.

6. The doctrine is contrary to the nature of divine grace, for grace truly enables man to exercise his will toward God in repentance and faith; whereas, according to this doctrine, grace takes away the freedom of the will and hinders its exercise. Further, the Scriptures present grace as something which man can resist (Acts 7:51; 2 Corinthians 6:1; Hebrews 12:15; Luke 7:30, etc.), but the Calvinistic doctrine declares grace to be irresistible.

7. The doctrine is dishonorable to Jesus Christ our Savior; for it declares that the decree of salvation was prior to the decree that Jesus should be the Savior. The Westminster Confession, for example, states, "As God hath appointed the elect unto glory, so hath he, by the eternal and most free purpose of his will, foreordained all the means thereto. Wherefore they who are elected being fallen in Adam, are redeemed by Christ... Neither are any other redeemed by Christ, effectually called, justified, adopted, sanctified, and saved, but the elect only."[16]

This confession plainly states that Jesus is introduced as a means to accomplish what God had already determined should be done. Such reduction of Jesus to a means to a predetermined end is most demeaning to Him. Arminius insisted that Jesus was the very foundation of election and not a subordinate cause of our salvation.

8. The doctrine is damaging to the biblical doctrine of salvation for sinful men; for if men sin through an unavoidable necessity by the decree of God, they cannot possibly manifest such a godly sorrow for their own sins as if they were personally responsible for them.

9. The doctrine inverts the order of the gospel; for, whereas the gospel says, "Believe, and thou shalt live," this doctrine says, "Since it is my will to give thee life, it is therefore my will to give thee faith."

10. The doctrine subverts the foundation of religion in general. According to true religion, God's love for men is expressed in keeping with His love for righteousness and His hatred for sin. That is, His love for men never supercedes His love for righteousness. According to this doctrine, however, His love for certain men and His hatred for others is prior to His love for righteousness, and He makes certain ones righteous and others sinful so that He can manifest His love and hatred for them respectively.

Wesley's Objection

John Wesley agreed essentially with Arminius in his condemnation of Calvinistic predestination. In his treatise on the question, "What is an Arminian?" he stated that the question of predestination marked the most important distinction between the Calvinists and the Arminians. He summarized as follows: "Is predestination absolute or conditional? The Arminians believe it is conditional; the Calvinists, that it is absolute."[17] By the term "conditional" he meant that only those who believe on the Lord Jesus Christ are predestined to salvation. Although Christ died for all men, it is predetermined that only those who believe on Him shall be saved.

Wesley added a forceful objection to the doctrine, stating that it overthrows the doctrine of saving faith as well as of judgment. In numerous scriptures the basis of salvation is declared to be faith in Christ. Unbelief is the basis for condemnation. (See Mark 16:16; John 3:36; Revelation 21:8, etc.) But if Jesus did not die to save those who are unconditionally reprobated from all eternity, how shall they be expected to believe on Him as their Savior? Shall they believe a lie, that He died for them, when in fact He did not? And shall they be condemned to eternal perdition because they do not believe that which is false? According to this doctrine men are required to believe what is not true; and if they do not believe it, they are everlastingly punished for not doing so! There could be no more unfair basis of judgment than this!

Implications

In treating the Calvinistic position, we noted three implications which are of the most vital importance. We must now see how the contrasting position views them.

First was the implication that *all sin has occurred by the decree of God.* It was probably against this idea that Arminius took his strongest stand of opposition; for, according to it, God is the author of sin. This is proven by four propositions:

1) God has absolutely decreed to demonstrate His glory by saving some men and damning others, the latter of which could not possibly be done unless sin had entered into the world.

2) In order to achieve His objective, God decreed that man should commit sin and become depraved, and the fall of man into sin followed by divine appointment.

3) God has by this scheme denied to the reprobate the measure of grace necessary for him to avoid sin, and this denial was decreed before man had ever sinned. It was thus utterly impossible for man in his created condition to avoid the fall into sin.

4) The operations of God in connection with predestination totally destroy the free will of men, inasmuch as it is totally impossible for man to avoid the decree which God has imposed upon him or to deliver himself from the state into which it was decreed he should fall; and, again, this decree was made before the man ever sinned.

> From these premises, we deduce... *that God really sins.* Because according to this doctrine, he moves to sin by an act that is unavoidable, and according to his own purpose and primary intention, without having received any previous inducement to such an act from any preceding sin or demerit in man.
>
> From the same position we might infer, that *God is the only sinner.* For man, who is impelled by an irresistible force to commit sin (that is, to perpetrate some deed that has been prohibited), cannot be said to sin himself.
>
> As a legitimate consequence, it also follows, *that sin is not sin,* since whatever that be which God does, it neither can be sin, nor ought any of his acts to receive that appellation.[18]

Calvinists have labored much to avoid such a conclusion. They revere God too highly to charge Him with sinfulness. What they do not seem to recognize is that their system of doctrine has within its logic the implicit conclusion that God is indeed the author of all sin. Take the following statement as an example of how Calvinists seek to avoid the necessary conclusion from their own logic.

> The apparent contradiction has been expressed this way: (a) God is the author of all that is. (b) Sin is. (c) Yet God is not the author of sin. But the contradiction is only apparent. For God s not the *author* of all that is, although he has decreed all. Satan and his host (of men and angels) are the "authors" of sin, although God has created them and decreed even their sin without being himself the author of it.[19]

This attempted evasion involves first, a misuse of words. The word "author" means "one who produces, creates, or brings into being; the beginner, creator, or first mover of anything."[20] It is evident, then, according to the Calvinists' own view of God's sovereignty, that He is the author of all that is or ever shall be. He is indeed the "beginner, creator, or first mover of everything."

The assertion that God is the source of decrees but not the author of events is a second violation of the Calvinist doctrine of sovereignty. The above-quoted author endeavors to relieve God of responsibility for sinful conduct by introducing free moral agents as secondary causes—as the authors of sin. Many other writers could be quoted who make the same effort. Yet, according to their own description of God's absolute sovereignty, it is not possible that any creature should act to thwart God's own effective purpose in the slightest way. Commenting on the controlling providence of God, the same author says,

> (1) that God, who created all things, also sustains them in being, (2) that he exercises over them complete control, (3) that this control regards all creatures and their actions as well as events in the natural world, (4) that this absolute control effects the execution of God's fixed plan, and (5) that all this has as its end the manifestation of the glory of God.[21]

Notice that, according to this conception, God absolutely controls every action of every creature and that those actions are the fulfillment of His fixed plan. Such a view of His absolute sovereignty simply does not allow secondary causes to enter and introduce actions contrary to God's plan. If His plan is being absolutely fulfilled, then He must be fully responsible for causing it to be so.

To illustrate further the inconsistency of the Calvinists in endeavoring to relieve God of any responsibility for sin, while at the same time maintaining His absolute sovereignty, we may examine the position of Charles Hodge, renowned theologian of the Reformed Church. Writing on the decrees of God, he stated,

> The universality of the decree flows from the universal dominion of God. What-

ever He does, He certainly purposed to do. Whatever He permits to occur, He certainly purposed to permit. Nothing can occur that was not foreseen, and if foreseen, it must have been intended. As the Scriptures teach that the providential control of God extends to all events, even the most minute, they do thereby teach that his decrees are equally comprehensive.[22]

It may be particularly observed that whether God acts, or permits others to act, the results are equally intended by Him.

In considering sinful acts, Hodge asserted,

With regard to the sinful acts of men, the Scriptures teach, (1) That they are so under the control of God that they can occur only by his permission and in execution of his purposes. He so guides them in the exercise of their wickedness that the particular forms of its manifestations are determined by his will... (4) The Scriptures teach that God's providence in relation to the sins of men, is such that the sinfulness thereof proceedeth only from the creature and not from God; who neither is nor can be the author or approver of sin.[23]

Hodge here claims that 1) sinners are under the control of God; 2) they are executing His purpose; 3) the particular form of wickedness is determined by His will; and yet that 4) such sinfulness proceedeth only from the creature; and that 5) God is not the author of sin.

Considering 5) first, and recalling the foregoing definition of "author," we are forced to say that in such a system, God is indeed made the author ("beginner, creator, or first mover") of sin. It begins in His sovereign purpose, and it is He who moves and guides sinners in the particular details of their conduct, so that they always fulfill His will. With regard to 4), it is evident that a contradiction is involved. If the action occurs under God's control, for the execution of His purpose, and with each detail determined by His will, it is surely impossible then to say that the action proceeds *only from the sinner*. True, it proceeds *immediately* from the sinner, but he is only an instrument for the accomplishment of God's sovereign purpose.

When Hodge came to consider the relation between God as the primary cause and sinners as the secondary cause of sin, he acknowledged the difficulty of his position. He spoke of the efficiency (directness or immediacy) of second causes and said, "He, as a free, personal, extra-mundane Being, controls the... efficiency of second causes, so as to determine their action according to his own will."[24] Applying the concept of efficiency to human actions, he wrote, "Why then should we attempt to explain how it is that the efficiency of God controls the efficiency of second causes? The fact is plain, and the fact alone is important; but the mode of God's action we cannot possibly understand."[25] The question may be restated as follows: if a sinner is directly responsible for a sinful action, how can we then say that God is directly responsible for controlling the sinner and producing that action through him? Both are true, Hodge said, though we cannot understand how. According to his theological system, God must predetermine and control every thought, desire and action of the sinner, while the sinner alone is responsible.

This is where Arminius turned back from following the Calvinistic system. He was convinced that if every sin came to pass strictly because of God's absolute decree, without any possible avoidance thereof, then God alone was responsible for sin. Ultimately, this makes Him the one and only sinner in the universe! Since Arminius could never accept such a conclusion, he rejected the faulty theological system that produced it. Wesleyans follow Arminius in this evaluation.

The second implication of Calvinism to be evaluated is *the predestination of non-elect infants to eternal damnation.* Wesleyan-Arminian theologians have consistently objected to this doctrine. Arminius held that, since Adam's transgression was pardoned, there is no reason to conclude that God imputed his sin to every infant. Sin is imputed to a person when he sins by his own choice.[26]

Richard Watson, early Wesleyan theologian, used Romans 5:18 as a scriptural basis for teaching that all children who die in infancy partake of the saving benefits of Christ's atonement. "Therefore, as by the offence of one judgment came upon all men to condemnation, even so by the righteousness of one the free gift came upon all men unto justification of life." Watson commented,

> If the whole human race be meant in the former clause, the whole human race is meant in the latter also; and it follows that as all are injured by the offence of Adam, so all are benefited by the obedience of Christ. Whatever, therefore, that benefit may be, all children dying in infancy must partake of it.[27]

We may not understand just how this justification is applied to infants, since they do inherit original sin, and since they are not actually regenerated when they are born. But the "free gift" is for all persons, and it is truly theirs until it is willfully rejected. It is only by rejecting the free gift that people perish, Watson affirmed. In this manner, the "dreadful decree" of Calvin's doctrine is happily avoided.

The third implication of Calvinism, concerning *the freedom of man*, has already been partially considered from the Arminian viewpoint. It is appropriate here to answer a criticism often directed against Arminians, that they teach salvation by works of the human will. Let the answer be in Arminius' own words:

> Free will is unable to begin or perfect any true and spiritual good, without grace ... I affirm, therefore, that this grace is simply and absolutely necessary for the illumination of the mind, the due ordering of the affections, and the inclination of the will to that which is good. It is this grace which operates on the mind, the affections, and the will; which infuses good thoughts into the mind, inspires good desires into the affections, and bends the will to carry into execution good thoughts and good desires...
>
> This grace commences salvation, promotes it, and perfects and consummates it...
>
> I confess that the mind of ... a natural and carnal man is obscure and dark, that his affections are corrupt and inordinate, that his will is stubborn and disobedient, and that the man himself is dead in sins. And I add to this—that teacher obtains my highest approbation who ascribes as much as possible to divine grace, provided he also pleads the cause of grace, as not to inflict an injury on the justice of God, and not to take away *the free will to that which is evil.*[28]

Most evidently, Arminius attributed nothing of salvation to the merit of human works or of will. If a man is saved, *it is all of grace*. It is grace that illuminates the mind, draws the affections, inclines and even "bends the will," and consummates the salvation in the individual. But this inclining and bending of the will does not destroy it. In evaluating the alternatives, a person, in spite of strong reasons and mighty benefits attracting toward salvation, can choose the lesser good and greater evil. If he is saved, he will declare it is because he has willingly yielded to the movings of grace. His will has added nothing to grace, but has received it as a gift. If he is lost, it is because he has chosen to refuse or resist it. The will is still free to choose evil, Arminius asserted. Wesley and a long line of theologians have agreed.

Two Bible characters may serve to illustrate the freedom of the will. They are chosen because their cases have so commonly been taken as illustrating God's compelling predestination to life and death, respectively. They are Saul of Tarsus and Pharaoh of Egypt.

The Case of Saul

Saul, who was converted on the Damascus road (Acts 9:1-9), is often said to have been saved because of irresistible grace. Pharaoh, on the contrary, is described as one who was hardened solely by the operation of God so that his destruction and reprobation could be more evident (Exodus, Chapters 5-14).

Concerning Saul, there is nothing in the initial account or in his succeeding descriptions of it which indicate he was irresistibly saved without the free concurrence of his will. Admittedly, there was a blinding revelation from heaven; but this came as the climax of a process of evaluation. Jesus said to the stricken man, "It is hard for thee to kick against the pricks" (Acts 9:5). Those words reveal that he was suffering from an intense inner conflict in which he was forced to reevaluate his position. On one hand, there was the witness of Stephen, as he was about to die a martyr's death, that he saw Jesus standing at the right hand of God (Acts 7:56). We can be sure this made a profound impression on Saul, for many years later when he faced death he repeated almost the exact words of Stephen concerning his enemies: "I pray God that it may not be laid to their charge" (Compare Acts 7:60 with 2 Timothy 4:16). As he journeyed toward Damascus, he was doubtless considering this impressive witness that Jesus was really in heaven.

On the other hand, there was his loyalty to the law and to his position in the Jewish community. The conflict was evidently disturbing and painful, like an ox kicking against the goad of its driver.

Then came the revelation from heaven and the words of Jesus Himself, "I am Jesus whom thou persecutest..." It was convincing evidence that Stephen's testimony was correct: Jesus is indeed in heaven! He is the Messiah! There was a physical manifestation of blinding light, but more important, there was convincing evidence of Who Jesus is. Paul was intellectually honest enough to submit to that evidence and reorder his life accordingly, regardless of what it might cost him.

That Paul was not irresistibly converted and commissioned is evident from his own words. When the revelation came, he did not know the identity of the divine speaker until he personally inquired, "Who art thou, Lord?" He did not know what was required of him until he asked,"Lord, what wilt thou have me to do?"

Paul was certainly conscious of the power and grace of God manifested in his conversion and call. At the same time, he recognized his own personal responsibility. When testifying before Agrippa, he said, "I was not disobedient unto the heavenly vision" (Acts 26:19). On God's part, there was the convincing revelation. On Paul's part, there was willing obedience. He continued by testifying, "Having therefore obtained help of God, I continue unto this day, witnessing..." On God's part, there was help or assistance, not an irresistible manifestation of power. On his own part, there was the determination to stand firm (continue) in the place of responsibility God appointed for him. He thus acknowledged both the indispensable enablement of God and his free and voluntary response.

John Peter Lange, writing from a Reformed background, commented thus on Paul's conversion. "The figurative expression [of "kicking against the pricks"] implied that Paul's own will, which offered resistance, would necessarily be subdued by the express command of the Redeemer, who appeared to him in overwhelming glory."[29] There was grace enough to convince the mind and move the will. That it was not irresistible, though, is taught in the following words from Lange:

> Did the Lord then compel him to retire on the course he had entered? By no means; for almighty grace does not take hold of us in opposition to our will, but it is precisely our will that takes hold of grace, so that we joyfully and unconditionally submit to it, having now distinctly seen the way of salvation.[30]

The Case of Pharaoh

In Pharaoh, king of Egypt, we have a contrasting case, for here was a man who stubbornly resisted God's grace and power. We may notice, first, that if God's demonstrations of power toward Saul of Tarsus are considered great enough to be irresistible, those toward Pharaoh should be considered equally so. They were equally convincing to the human mind, and they were much more numerous. At the first, Pharaoh said arrogantly, "Who is the Lord, that I should obey his voice to let Israel go? I know not the Lord, neither will I let Israel go" (Exodus 5:2). During the ensuing plagues, he was convinced of who God is. He confessed, "I have sinned this time: the LORD is righteous, and I and my people are wicked" (Exodus 9:27).

For Pharaoh, as for Saul, there was intense conflict as he weighed the alternatives. On one hand, there was conclusive evidence that he was confronting Jehovah, the God of heaven. His priests confessed, "This is the finger of God" (Exodus 8:19). His servants pleaded, "Let the men go, that they may serve the Lord their God: knowest thou not yet that Egypt is destroyed?" (Exodus 10:7). At the death of their firstborn, the people arose *en masse*, crying, "We are all dead men," and urged the Israelites to leave hastily (Exodus 12:33). For a while Pharaoh was swept along with this mass movement. But when he realized this vast army of slaves was actually on the march, he reconsidered. What would become of his mighty building projects? How could he endure the loss of so many valuable workers? Within the deliberations of his own mind Pharaoh reached a decision: he would pursue the Israelites and bring them back.

The cases of Saul and Pharaoh illustrate an important principle: God sends grace to men sufficient to enlighten their mind and move their wills. At the same time, He supplies—yes, even insures—strength sufficient for their wills to resist in spite of all the intellectual and moral force applied through grace. Saul could have resisted, as is strongly suggested in his words, "I was not disobedient to the heavenly vision." It appears that even more powerful influence toward repentance was applied to Pharaoh. But God will not coerce the will of any man; so he gave sufficient courage[31] to Pharaoh's heart to resist if he chose. And he did choose, of his own will, to resist, even unto his own destruction and that of his army!

"Predestination" Analyzed

It is appropriate to study the word "predestination," as it is understood by Wesleyan-Arminians. "Predestinate" comes from two Greek words, *pro* and *orizo*. *Pro* means "in advance," and *orizo* means to appoint, determine, or to set limits. Two meanings of *orizo* are given by Arndt and Gingrich in their authoritative lexicon: "1. Determine, appoint, fix, set... 2. set limits to, define, explain..."[32] Thus to predestinate means to determine, fix, define or set limits, in advance. The word does not inherently refer to persons or their eternal destiny. We must discover from an honest study of scriptures what is being set, determined, or limited in advance.

A great number of Bible passages assures us that God did not determine from all eternity who must be eternally saved and who eternally damned, without any foreknowledge of their character or response to the gospel. John Wesley used many of these passages in his teaching about predestination. For example, he stressed Ezekiel 33:11 ("As I live, saith the Lord God, I have no pleasure in the death of the wicked; but that the wicked turn from his way and live: turn ye, turn ye from your evil ways; for why will ye die, O house of Israel?"), and 1 Timothy 2:4 ("Who [God] will have all men to be saved, and to come unto the knowledge of the truth.")[33] No scripture teaches the contrary: that God determines from all eternity to damn certain individuals.

Concerning the proper concept of predestination, Arminius wrote as follows:

> It is the foreordination of sinners who shall believe in Christ to eternal life, and on the contrary, the predamnation of sinners who shall persevere in sins to eternal death; *who shall believe*, through the gracious gift of God, and *who shall persevere in sins* through their own wickedness and the just desertion of God.[34]

Wesley amplified this view by declaring that predestination involved God's prearranged plan to save those who should believe on Jesus Christ as their Savior, and persist in such faith, and to damn those who persist in unbelief.[35]

This discussion may be concluded with consideration of some of the Bible passages where predestination and related terms are considered. The Greek word occurs in Acts 4:28; Romans 8:29-30; 1 Corinthians 2:7; and Ephesians 1:5, 11. The Romans and Ephesians passages are the most vital to our study.

Romans 8:29-30 says, "For whom he did foreknow, he also did predestinate to be conformed to the image of his Son, that he might be the firstborn among many brethren. Moreover whom he did predestinate, them he also called: and whom he called, them he also justified; and whom he justified, them he also glorified."

We may observe, first, that God's predestination is according to His foreknowledge and not vice versa, as Calvinists have claimed. Although a different term is used, the same order may be seen in 1 Peter 1:2, where the saints are said to be "elect according to the foreknowledge of God the Father…"

Observe, moreover, that predestination is not said to be unto eternal life or eternal damnation. It rather concerns our conformity to Jesus Christ.

Here is, in summary, Wesley's comment on the passage:

> As all that are called were predestinated, so all whom God has predestinated he foreknew. He knew, he saw them as believers, and as such predestinated them to salvation, according to his eternal decree, "He that believeth shall be saved." Thus we see the whole process of the work of God, from the end to the beginning. Who are glorified? None but those who are first sanctified. Who are sanctified? None but those who were first justified. Who are justified? None but those who were first predestinated. Who are predestinated? None but those whom God foreknew as believers. Thus the purpose and word of God stand unshaken as the pillars of heaven: "He that believeth shall be saved; he that believeth not shall be damned."[36]

Watson clearly showed that the predestination spoken of in this passage is personal and individual and that it applies to those who believe in Christ. He referred to Romans 11:2 for the meaning of "foreknown": "God hath not cast away his people which he foreknew." He explained, "It is not of the whole people of Israel of which the apostle here speaks, as the context shows; but of the believing part of them, called subsequently 'the remnant according to the election of grace.'"[37] He further showed that those who are foreknown (v. 29) are the same ones who "love God… who are the called according to His purpose" (v. 28). God's foreknowledge is then based on a real distinction between the objects of predestination and other people. "It is their faith itself: for of believers only is St. Paul speaking as the subjects of this foreknowledge; and such believers too who "love God."[38]

This discussion should assist us in understanding Ephesians 1:4, 5, 11 also: "According as he hath chosen us in him before the foundation of the world, that we should be holy and without blame before him in love: having predestinated us unto the adoption of children by Jesus Christ to himself, according to the good pleasure of his will... In whom also we have obtained an inheritance, being predestinated according to the purpose of him who worketh all things after the counsel of his own will..." The word *counsel* signifies intelligent deliberation. There was good reason for God's choice of some men to blessings, as Watson explained:

> The conclusion is inevitable that those whom he chose in Christ "before the foundation of the world," were considered, not as *men* merely, which gives no reason of choice worthy of any rational being, much less of the ever blessed God; but as believing men, which harmonizes the doctrine of election with the other doctrines of Scripture, instead of placing it, as in opposition to them.[39]

In neither of the passages is predestination unto eternal life or eternal perdition; it is, rather, to certain other benefits which come to believers in Christ. In Romans 8:29 it is conformity to the image of God's Son, especially that likeness which we shall enjoy when we are glorified. In Ephesians 1:5 it is unto the adoption of children. St. Paul is surely not talking of God's arbitrary choosing of some men for heaven and some for hell without any basis whatever seen in the individuals chosen.

One more passage, while it does not contain the word *predestined,* is often used in an effort to prove the Calvinistic position, and it needs to be considered. Acts 13:48 speaks of the response to St. Paul's preaching in Antioch and says, "as many as were ordained to eternal life believed." The Greek word for *ordained* is *tasso* and is not contained in the words for predestination. It has no reference to anything done in advance, as if God had predetermined who should believe and be saved. The word means to arrange, set, appoint, frame, order or dispose.[40] "It has been considered here as implying the *disposition* or *readiness of mind* of several persons in the congregation, such as the *religious proselytes* mentioned in verse 43, who possessed the reverse of the *disposition* of those Jews who spoke *against those things, contradicting and blaspheming*, verse 45."[41] Just as a person who arranges or is disposed to travel the expressway from Seoul to Pusan in Korea must go through Taegu, so must a person who is disposed to be saved reach that salvation by the exercise of faith. There is no other way. Those Jews who would not believe could not gain eternal life. Paul and Barnabas said, "Seeing ye put [the Word of God] from you, and judge yourselves unworthy of everlasting life, lo, we turn to the Gentiles" (Acts 13:46). Among those Gentiles were many who were disposed to eternal life, and they laid hold of it by faith. We recognize, of course, that the inner disposition to gain eternal life came not from sinful man himself, but by the gracious operation of the Holy Spirit. Nevertheless, it was not merely the sovereign act of God apart from a willing human response that brought faith and salvation. People believed in Christ because they saw Him as the fulfillment of prophecy and God's appointed way of salvation.

In summary, we may say that predestination refers to the setting of limits or the fixing of plans and purposes in advance. Concerning salvation, it refers to God's plan and purpose to save men from ruin through sin. His plan is to save those who place their trust in Jesus Christ and to allow others to be lost through unbelief. His decree is expressed in Mark 16:16, "He that believeth and is baptized shall be saved; but he that believeth not shall be damned." We can never be saved apart from the operation of divine grace; but even with the boundless measure of grace moving toward us from the heart of God, there is no salvation unless we believe in Jesus Christ with all our hearts. It is God's predestinated plan, and we must accommodate ourselves to it or be lost.

Endnotes

1. *Institutes*, III:xxiii:6.
2. *Ibid.*, III:xxi:5.
3. *Ibid.*, III:xxiii:7
4. *Ibid.*, III:xxiii:8.
5. *Ibid.*, III:xxiii:7.
6. *Westminster Confession of Faith*, Section VI: Paragraphs 1, 3. Hereafter referred to in the form "*Westminster*, VI:1, 3." The Confession was produced by the famous Westminster Assembly in England (1643-1649) and has long been regarded as one of the most complete and systematic statements of Calvinism ever to be produced. It served for many years as the basis of faith for Presbyterian and Reformed churches.
7. John H. Gerstner, *A Predestination Primer* (Winona Lake, IN: Alpha Publications, 1979), p. 30.
8. *Institutes*, III:xxi:5.
9. Gerstner, *Op. cit.*, p. 31.
10. Pentecost, *Op. cit.*, pp. 138-39.
11. Wiley, *Op. cit.*, I, p. 357.
12. Arminius, *Op. cit.*, III, pp. 66-67.

13. Richard Watson, *Theological Institutes* (New York: Nelson and Phillips, 1850), Vol. I, p. 380.

14. Arminius, *Op. cit.*, pp. 216-17.

15. *Westminster*, III:6.

16. Wesley, *Works*, X, p. 360.

17. Arminius, *Op. cit.*, I, p. 229.

18. G. I. Williamson, *The Westminster Confession of Faith for Study Classes* (Philadelphia: The Presbyterian and Reformed Publishing Co., 1964), p. 50.

19. *Webster's New Twentieth Century Dictionary*, Second Edition (Collins-World Publishing Co., 1975), p. 126.

20. Williamson, *Op. cit.*, p. 46.

21. Charles Hodge, *Systematic Theology* (Grand Rapids, MI: Wm. B. Eerdmans Publishing Co., 1968 reprint), Vol. I, pp. 542-43.

22. *Ibid.*, pp. 589-90.

23. *Ibid.*, Vol. II, p. 665.

24. *Ibid.*, Vol. I, p. 605.

25. Arminius, *Op. cit.*, Vol. I, p. 319.

26. Watson, *Op. cit.*, Vol. II, pp. 57-58.

27. Arminius, *Op. cit.*, Vol. II, pp. 472-73.

28. John Peter Lange, *Commentary on the Holy Scriptures* (Grand Rapids, MI: Zondervan Publishing House, n.d. edition), Vol. on Acts, p. 442.

29. *Ibid.*, p. 174.

30. It will be shown in Chapter 8 that the word "harden" applied to Pharaoh's heart means to embolden or encourage.

31. William F. Arndt and F. Wilbur Gingrich, *A Greek-English Lexicon of the New Testament*, translated and adapted from the German original by Walter Bauer (Chicago: The University of Chicago Press, 1957), p. 584.

32. Wesley also emphasized such passages as Col. 1:28; Hebrews 2:9; John 3:17; 12:47; 2 Peter 2:3, 9; I John 2:1, 2; Psalm 17:14; Isaiah 13:11; Matthew 18:7; John 2:7, 8, 26; 12:19; 14:17; 15:18, 19; 18:20; 1 Corinthians 1:21; 2:12; 6:2; Galatians 6:14; James 1:27; 2 Peter 2:20; I John 2:15; 3:1; 4:4, 5.

33. Arminius, *Op. cit.*, Vol. III, p. 292.

34. Wesley, *Works*, Vol. VI, p. 229.

35. *Ibid.*

36. Watson, *Op. cit.*, Vol. II, p. 357.

37. *Ibid.*, p. 358

38 *Ibid.*, p. 350.

39. Harold K. Moulton, ed., *The Analytical Greek Lexicon Revised* (Grand Rapids, MI: Zondervan Publishing House, 1978), p. 398.

40. Beacon Bible Commentary (Kansas City, MO: Beacon Hill Press, 1965), Vol. VII, p. 414.

4

Election

Closely related to the theme of the last chapter is the truth of election. The latter term, however, indicates a choice, whereas the other does not. In His electing work, God chose whom He would save and upon what basis. Election is thus subordinate to predestination, which includes the general plan of salvation and the rewards to which the elect are called.

Election is usually considered in contrast with reprobation, the former being choice unto salvation, and the latter unto damnation. Those chosen are called the elect and the reprobate, respectively. Both choices are branches of God's plan for mankind expressed in predestination.

The Strong Calvinistic View

Book III, Chapter 21, in Calvin's *Institutes* is titled as follows: "Of the eternal election, by which God has predestined some to salvation, and others to destruction." In the chapter Calvin explained his position thus:

> God by his eternal and immutable counsel determined once for all those whom it was his pleasure one day to admit to salvation, and those whom, on the other hand, it was his pleasure to doom to destruction. We maintain that his counsel, as regards the elect, is founded on free mercy, without any respect to human worth, while those whom he dooms to destruction are excluded from access to life by a just and blameless, but at the same time incomprehensible judgment.[1]

It may immediately be observed that this view of election follows from the foregoing positions relative to God's sovereignty and His predestination. If we view God in His sovereignty as predetermining all events whatever without any regard for influences outside Himself, then we must, to be logically consistent, accept the fact of God's electing some people to salvation and others to damnation, without any consideration of what they shall ever be or do in themselves.

Types of Election

Some observations should be made concerning this strong concept of election. First, it does not adequately distinguish between the numerous types of election presented in the Word. These will be discussed later in the chapter. We may illustrate here by showing Calvin's failure to differentiate between national and individual election. He said:

> All are not created on equal terms, but some are preordained to eternal life, others to eternal damnation; and accordingly, as each has been created for one or other of these ends, we say that he has been predestinated to life or to death. This God has testified, not only in the case of single individuals; he has also given a specimen of it in the whole posterity of Abraham, to make it plain that the future condition of each nation was entirely at his disposal.[2]

It is surely true that God did choose the offspring of Abraham for a special purpose, but the eternal salvation of each individual was not thereby determined. Multitudes of individual Israelites have been spiritually lost, though born into an elect nation. Similarly, great multitudes have been individually saved, though not born in an elect nation. The two kinds of election have reference to different ends.

The Partiality of Election

Second, the means of grace and salvation are in this view imposed upon the individual by the Lord God, without reference to anything in that person which might distinguish him from the reprobate. Nothing of faith, obedience or receptiveness within the person prepares him for election; these qualities are rather bestowed arbitrarily upon the elect and withheld from the reprobate. Such a concept raises the most serious questions about the sincerity and justice of God, which the Calvinists are never able adequately to answer. How can a God of sincere love and faithful justice arbitrarily cause some to be saved eternally while others are condemned to hell eternally, without regard to anything in those individuals which would distinguish the one from the other? Calvin recognized that there was no adequate explanation for such arbitrary and extreme actions attributed to God. He fought against the efforts of rational men to demand justification for such distorted views of God. Of those who would persist in seeking answers, he said,

> When they inquire into predestination, let them remember that they are penetrating into the recess of the divine wisdom, where he who rushes forward securely and confidently instead of satisfying his curiosity will enter an inextricable labyrinth. For it is not right that man should with impunity pry into things which the Lord has been pleased to conceal within himself, and scan that sublime eternal

> wisdom which it is his pleasure that we should not apprehend but adore, that therein also his perfections may appear.
>
> ...Let us not be ashamed to be ignorant in a matter in which ignorance is learning. Rather let us willingly abstain from the search after knowledge, to which it is both foolish as well as perilous, and even fatal to aspire... There is good reason to dread presumption which can only plunge us headlong into ruin.[3]

Let us view more closely this elective activity of God. Looking upon the persons He has made, He chooses some to be recipients of eternal blessedness and others to languish forever in flames of hell, without there being the slightest difference between those creatures of His, upon which such a distinction can be justified or by which it can be explained. If we should see parents treating their children that way, we would with one consent condemn them for heartless and cruel partiality. If teachers should subject their students to such arbitrary discrimination, they would be summarily dismissed, for good reason. But when God is presented as doing thus, with eternal consequences flowing from His actions, we are asked to believe that His perfection is now appearing. We must not ask why, Calvin insists, but count ignorance to be learning. We must adore God for doing what we would condemn in our fellowmen. A character which would be horrifying in an earthly ruler is to be deemed as sublime when hidden away in the inscrutable heart of God!

Let it be emphatically declared that we are not belittling God in saying such things. We are rather exposing the unreasonableness of a doctrine which so distorts the character of God.

The Mild Calvinistic View

A large and increasing number of people have been appalled at the doctrine of unconditional election, with the implications which have been presented above. Consequently, a moderate position has been formulated to remove that which is so offensive in strong Calvinism. To alleviate the stigma of partiality which has been attached to God, this mild system does require something on the part of the person who is to be saved. There must be an act of faith in Christ if salvation is to come to the sinner.

A Logical Deficiency

While removing one difficulty, this position of doctrine introduces another one just as serious. Up to this point the logic of the Calvinistic system has been quite consistent, though with some exceptions which have been pointed out.

By introducing this human condition into the message of election, though, the logical system is broken: it is no longer consistent. For if a person must believe in order to be saved, then it is possible for a mere man to thwart the will of God, and God is thus robbed of His sovereignty, as it is described in Calvinistic doctrine. Moreover, if faith is necessary for salvation, then it may be possible for a person to believe at one time unto salvation and later to fall into unbelief and be lost. This is too great a departure from Calvin, even for the mild Calvinists. So they have introduced the strange teaching that, although a person must believe in order to be saved, he does not need to keep on believing in order to remain saved.

Such a position contradicts the clear teaching of scriptures that faith is necessary not only as an initial act bringing justification, but as a continuing practice to maintain justification. "The just shall live by faith" is a dictum often repeated in the Word (Habakkuk 2:4; Galatians 3:11; etc.). In the great majority of instances when faith is related to salvation in the New Testament, it is an ongoing faith and not just a one-time act.

A Moral Danger

The mild position is more dangerous than the other in that it encourages a very casual attitude toward sin in the life of the professing Christian. Once a person believes in Christ, so it is said, no amount of sin, disobedience and unbelief can ever alter that relationship to Him. The strong Calvinists have maintained a much higher regard for holiness of life than is commonly produced within the mild teaching. Calvin said, "Not only does faith, full and perfect faith, but all correct knowledge of God, originate in obedience."[4] He further allowed that one's assurance of his own election finally depends on his perseverance in faith. Hodge came to a similar conclusion. He remarked, "The only evidence of election is effectual calling, that is, the production of holiness."[5]

We thus find it necessary to reject the Calvinistic notion of election which, as we shall see, does not involve a proper understanding of Scripture concerning the subject.

The Wesleyan-Arminian View

Types of Election

The theme of election occurs many times in the Bible, but it is impossible to gain a proper understanding of it unless we recognize that there are several types of election, and they do not all refer to eternal salvation. We need to see five aspects of the theme.

1) There is, first, the election of Christ. Matthew took a key passage from Isaiah and applied it to Jesus: "Behold my servant, whom I uphold; mine elect, in whom my soul delighteth; I have put my spirit upon him: he shall bring forth judgment to the Gentiles" (Isaiah 42:1; cf Matthew 12:18). St. Peter took another passage from Isaiah and applied it to Jesus: "Wherefore also it is contained in the scripture, Behold, I lay in Sion a chief cornerstone, elect, precious: and he that believeth on him shall not be confounded. Unto you therefore which believe he is precious; but unto them which be disobedient, the stone which the builders disallowed, the same is made the head of the corner" (1 Peter 2:6-7; cf Isaiah 28:16).

Jesus was not chosen of God to be saved, but to be the Savior of all who would believe in Him. God's election of His Son as the Messiah, the Savior, is absolutely central and primary in the whole theme of redemption. No other person can ever be elected unto salvation except through Him. St. Paul's crucial passage on election and predestination (Ephesians 1:3-12), which is all one extended sentence, contains an unmistakable emphasis on the centrality of Christ. The phrase "in Christ," or something similar to it, occurs nine times in the passage. All spiritual blessings are *in Him*; we have been chosen *in Him*; we have been predestined unto adoption *by Him*; we have been made accepted *in the Beloved*; *in Him* we have redemption *through His blood*; God's purpose is to gather all in one *in Christ; in Him* we have an inheritance; and all of this is for the purpose that we should be to the praise of His glory, who first trusted *in Christ.* This is God's predestination, settled after His own purpose and the counsel of His own will, that every blessing we receive is in and through Jesus Christ, the Elected One.

2) There is the election of nations or other groups of men to special place or privilege. The primary example is Israel. Isaiah 45:4 says, "For Jacob my servant's sake, and Israel mine elect..." Two things should be noticed about this election. First, it is a corporate, and not just an individual, election. True, when God made a choice between Jacob and Esau, the two were individual brothers. But at that very time, it was made plain that God was choosing one nation over another. The Lord said to Rebekah, "Two nations are in thy womb, and two manner of people shall be separated from thy bowels: and the one shall be stronger than the other people; and the elder shall serve the younger" (Genesis 25:23). This prophecy

was not fulfilled in the boys themselves, for Esau did not serve Jacob. Its fulfillment is in the two nations which came from them.

Second, it is an election to service and not to salvation. Isaiah 44:1 includes the same thought as the verse already given, that of election to service: "Hear, O Jacob my servant; and Israel, whom I have chosen." Israel was chosen to be a "kingdom of priests" (Exodus 19:6), to mediate between their God and other nations. Through Isaiah the Lord said, "Ye are my witnesses... that I am God... This people have I formed for myself; they shall show forth my praise" (Isaiah 43:10, 12, 21). St. Paul spoke of the high privileges of his kinsmen, "who are Israelites, to whom pertaineth the adoption, and the glory, and the covenants, and the giving of the law, and the service of God, and the promises; whose are the fathers, and of whom concerning the flesh Christ came" (Romans 9:4-5). It is noticeable that in that list of benefits he did not include eternal salvation.

In New Testament times the Jews commonly believed that salvation was assured unto them just because they were children of Abraham. John the Baptist encountered this concept as he preached, so he commanded, "Bring forth therefore fruits worthy of repentance, and begin not to say within yourselves, We have Abraham to our father: for I say unto you, That God is able of these stones to raise up children unto Abraham" (Luke 3:8). To put it bluntly, Jews considered simply as biological descendants from Abraham have no more right to eternal salvation than the stones by the river bank! Both are formed by physical processes. Salvation is a spiritual production, brought about through repentance and faith in Christ.

St. Paul insisted on the same truth. "For they are not all Israel, which are of Israel:... What shall we say then? That the Gentiles, which followed not after righteousness, have attained to righteousness, even the righteousness which is by faith. But Israel, which followed after the law of righteousness, hath not attained to the law of righteousness. Wherefore? Because they sought it not by faith, but as it were by the works of the law. For they stumbled at that stumblingstone; As it is written, Behold I lay in Sion a stumblingstone and rock of offence; and whosoever believeth on him shall not be ashamed" (Romans 9:6, 30-33). In Galatians 3:7 he said, "Know ye therefore that they which are of faith, the same are the children of Abraham." Unbelieving Israelites cannot find salvation, and believing Gentiles can find it: this was the startling truth which Paul declared to his people.

Some have argued strongly that when God chose between Jacob and Esau, the choice involved personal salvation; and they use the words of Malachi 1:1-2, "I loved Jacob, and I hated Esau," to establish their position. It must be recognized that when God expressed those words, the two persons named had long been dead; for they were first spoken through Malachi, the latest of the Old Testament prophets. It is perfectly evident that God was comparing the two nations, for He said of Edom, or Esau, "They shall call them,... The people against whom the Lord hath indignation forever" (Malachi 1:4). A little study of the Edomites will reveal why God had such indignation against them: they were a profane and rebellious people.

3) There is an individual election to office or responsibility, both within and without the nation of Israel. God initiated the nation of Israel by choosing Abraham, Isaac and Jacob (Nehemiah 9:7; Romans 9:7, 13). He chose Moses to lead them (Psalm 106:23), and David to rule them (Psalm 78:70), and Cyrus a Gentile to deliver them (Isaiah 45:1). He chose the Twelve to be messengers of the New Covenant (John 6:70). It is most obvious that personal salvation was not thereby assured, for Jesus said, "Have not I chosen you twelve, and one of you is a devil?" If the choosing guaranteed eternal life, we must then conclude that when "Judas by transgression fell, that he might go to his own place" (Acts 1:25), his place was in heaven. Such a conclusion is unthinkable. We must then allow that the election, even of apostles, did not assure final salvation.

4) There is the election of the Church as God's spiritual Israel. It is widely accepted that when Paul spoke of "we... who first trusted in Christ" (Ephesians 1:12), he referred to himself and other believing Israelites. He immediately followed by adding, "In whom ye also trusted, after that ye heard the word of truth, the gospel of your salvation." The *ye* is identified in 2:11, 13, "ye being in time past Gentiles in the flesh... But now in Christ Jesus ye who sometimes were far off are made nigh by the blood of Christ." The long-concealed mystery which St. Paul so gladly proclaimed was that in Christ Jesus both Jews and Gentiles are made one, and this one body is the Church (Ephesians 2:19-22; 3:8-11).

Like the original Israel, this one is elect in a corporate sense. Robert Shank, who after intense study turned from his mildly Calvinistic background to embrace an Arminian position, wrote,

> The election to salvation is *corporate* as well as Christocentric. The corporate nature of election has been noted by many. In his comment on Ephesians 1:4, previously cited, Lightfoot writes, "The election of Christ involves implicitly the election of the Church." Westcott comments on Ephesians 1:4, "*exelexato—He chose us* (i.e. Christians as a body v. 3) for Himself out of the world." Bloomfield

comments on Ephesians 1:5, "...the Apostle has here no reference to the *personal* election of *individuals*..."[6]

Forster and Marston stated the same conclusion after an intensive study of the Scriptures:

> The prime point is that the election of the church is a corporate rather than an individual thing. It is not that individuals are in the church because they are elect, it is rather that they are elect because they are in the church, which is the body of the elect One. Ruth was not chosen to become an Israelite but in becoming an Israelite, she partook of Israel's election.[7]

The significance of this corporateness of election lies in the fact that, whereas the church is fully assured of ultimate triumph, the believer's election as an individual is conditioned on faith and obedience. The subject will be studied further in the chapter on perseverance. It is analogous to the case of Israel: the nation was assured of continuing existence; individuals could be cut off and lost.

5) There is individual election unto salvation. Romans 16:13 speaks of a certain man, Rufus, who was "chosen in the Lord." He was not chosen or elected *to be* in the Lord, but as being in the Lord. He was a part of the elect body, but he was chosen individually. In his first epistle, Peter addressed persons in specific places as "elect according to the foreknowledge of God the Father, through sanctification of the Spirit..." (1 Peter 1:2). God foreknew who would be sanctified through the Spirit. They are the elect ones, individually, as they appropriate the sanctifying work of the Spirit.

Requirements of Personal Election

We should stress the fact that *personal election is in Christ.* Calvinism makes Christ secondary to God's sovereign, unconditional election of individuals and instrumental in accomplishing that election. Arminianism declares that He is central and primary in election. He is God's Elect, and individuals are elect only in Him. Yet their election is individual and personal. Arminius said, "No one is elect, except in Christ, as dead and risen again, and now constituted by God the Head of the church, and the Savior of them who should believe in him, and obey him unto Salvation."[8]

Again, let us observe that *personal election is conditional.* There are conditions which an individual must meet to be in Christ, and thus to be elected in Him. We are elect *in Him,* and not *to be in Him.* God foreknows who shall believe in Christ and He considers them the elect ones.

Already it has been shown that the election spoken of in Ephesians, Chapter 1, is corporate. Even if the passage were taken as applying to individual election, it would still be the case that election is by faith in Christ. Paul says we are "predestinated according to the purpose of him who worketh all things after the counsel of his own will: that we should be to the praise of his glory who first trusted in Christ" (vv. 11-12). There is no suggestion here that God's election is sheer divine will power working without purpose or reason. It is after "the counsel of his own will." There is wisdom and reason behind God's choice. The wise purpose is immediately made known, for the *we* who have obtained the inheritance according to predestination are those who first trusted in Christ. And others who later trust in Christ are also brought to share in the same benefits, as the following verses indicate.

Because election is conditional, Peter could say, "Wherefore the rather, brethren, give diligence to make your calling and election sure: for if ye do these things, ye shall never fall" (2 Peter 1:12). Such an exhortation to make election sure is entirely inconsistent with the Calvinistic idea of unconditional election of certain individuals to eternal life.

St. Peter wrote more about the election of the Church than any other New Testament writer, and he stressed the close analogy between the church and Israel. He said, "Ye are a chosen generation, a royal priesthood, an holy nation, a peculiar people; that ye should show forth the praises of him who hath called you out of darkness into his marvelous light: which in time past were not a people, but are now the people of God: which had not obtained mercy, but now have obtained mercy" (1 Peter 2:9-10). Similar statements about the nation of Israel can be found in numerous passages of Scripture, such as Exodus 19:5-6 and Isaiah 43:21. Just as individuals could be cut off from the nation of Israel and lose all of the benefits pertaining to the nation, so can individuals be cut off from the Church and lose the benefits of the Body of Christ.

Consideration of Additional Scripture Passages

A number of texts have already been examined in the present chapter. There are some others which have been interpreted as giving support to unconditional election, which we now will investigate.

The first one is John 15:16, spoken by Jesus to His disciples: "Ye have not chosen me, but I have chosen you, and ordained you, that ye should go and bring forth fruit, and that your fruit should remain." Calvin wrote as follows:

> Assuredly divine grace would not deserve all the praise of election, were not election gratuitous; and it would not be gratuitous, did God in electing any individual pay regard to his future works. Hence, what Christ said to his disciples is found universally applicable to all believers, "Ye have not chosen me, but I have chosen you."[9]

He thus applied the verse universally to individual believers. The inconsistency of this view is made manifest by Calvin's own treatment of a similar passage, John 6:70, "Have not I chosen you twelve, and one of you is a devil?" On this he said,

> In elsewhere numbering Judas among the elect, though he were a devil (John 6:70), he refers only to the apostolic office, which, though a bright manifestation of divine favor... does not however contain within itself the hope of eternal salvation.[10]

Calvin is correct in acknowledging that this passage refers to election unto apostolic office. He is incorrect in not treating the other passage in the same way. The entire message of John, chapters 13 to 16, was spoken in a closed session with His disciples. It began in the upper room at the time of the last supper. We should remember that the word "apostle" means "sent one." In this session Jesus was preparing them to be sent as special messengers of His. So in 13:16 He said, "The servant is not greater than his lord: neither he that is sent greater than he that sent him." In 15:3 Jesus said, "Now are ye clean through the word which I have spoken unto you." This surely refers back to the scene at the last supper when Jesus washed their feet and said, "And ye are clean, but not all." The exception was Judas, who in the meantime had left the company. After his departure Jesus could truly say, "Now ye are clean." It is in the same context that He said, "Ye have not chosen me, but I have chosen you, and ordained you, that ye should go and bring forth fruit." His sending of apostles is still plainly in view. He is not speaking of individual election unto salvation at all, but of their being chosen to the apostolic office.

Another passage often used to further the doctrine of unconditional election is 2 Thessalonians 2:13-14, "But we are bound to give thanks alway to God for you, brethren beloved of the Lord, because God hath from the beginning chosen you to salvation through sanctification of the Spirit and belief of the truth: whereunto he called you by our gospel, to the obtaining of the glory of our Lord Jesus Christ." Numerous writers have interpreted this as eternal election effected through the operation of the Spirit, irresistibly producing faith and sanctification.

We will concentrate on three key phrases: "from the beginning," "chosen," and "through... belief of the truth." The first phrase is uncertain in its exact meaning, as early manuscripts contain two different expressions. One means "firstfruits," and the other, as translated above, means "from the beginning." If the former is correct, Paul was addressing the "first converts" of Thessalonica, and the passage has no reference to God's eternal election. If "from the beginning" is correct, then we must understand how Paul uses the expression. It is not the same phrase which he uses in Ephesians 1:4 to denote something before the foundation of the world. There he uses the preposition *pro*, meaning "before." In the present passage he uses *ap*, which means "from" or "since." There are only two other places where Paul uses the same expression with reference to time. The first is Acts 26:4, "My manner of life from my youth, which was at the first among mine own nation at Jerusalem, know all the Jews." Here the same phrase is translated "at the first," and refers to his first days in Jerusalem. The other passage is in Philippians 4:15, "Now ye Philippians know also, that in the beginning of the gospel, when I departed from Macedonia, no church communicated with me as concerning giving and receiving, but ye only." Here "in the beginning" is identified as the time when he departed from Macedonia and left that infant church behind. In neither place does Paul have any thought of "from eternity past." It is reasonable to assume that his thought is the same in writing to the Thessalonians Upon Paul's first entrance into Thessalonica, there were remarkable effects from the preaching of the Word. Some believed and became exemplary witnesses for Christ. Others were stubbornly set against the gospel. These to whom the Apostle was writing were outstanding believers "from the beginning"—that is, from the first time they heard the gospel message.

The second key word is "chosen." The original is not the same as is commonly used for the "elect." The word is *haireomai*, which means the taking of one path instead of another. From the same root comes the common term for a separated group or sect. The meaning seems to be that while many in Thessalonica were resistant to truth, these believers were led of God apart from the rest into the way of salvation.

The third key expression is "through... belief of the truth." In contrast to the truth-rejecters "who received not the love of the truth, that they might be saved, and... believed not the truth, but had pleasure in unrighteousness," these did believe and love the truth, and were brought unto salvation by believing. They were not chosen *unto* faith, but *in or through* faith.

After a thorough study of the passage, Forster and Marston write,

> In summary, we take its meaning to be that from the beginning God divided off those who were willing to repent and believe in the truth, from those who preferred unrighteousness. The true believers have God's word working powerfully among them; the false follow the pretended signs and wonders that Satan energizes.[11]

The final passage to be studied is 2 Timothy 1:9-10, "[God] hath saved us, and called us with an holy calling, not according to our works, but according to his own purpose and grace, which was given us in Christ Jesus before the world began, but is now made manifest by the appearing of our Savior Jesus Christ, who hath abolished death, and hath brought life and immortality to light through the gospel." Calvin taught from these words that divine election was made without foresight of human actions, and that every virtue was a result of election.

It will quickly be observed that there is no reference to election in the passage, although the calling of God does occur. The purpose of Paul in writing this epistle was to inspire young Timothy for his difficult task of opposing heresies and other difficulties in Ephesus. He was challenged to "stir up the gift" that was in him. He was reminded that "God hath not given us the spirit of fear; but of power, and of love, and of a sound mind" (vv. 6-7); and he was encouraged to be a "partaker of the afflictions of the gospel according to the power of God' (v. 8). Then comes the reminder of our holy calling, in the text under consideration. Of that calling Barclay has said, "The gospel is not simply a rescue from the consequences and the penalty of past sin. The gospel is a summons to walk the way of holiness. The sheer, changing power of the gospel is a fact which is beyond argument."[12] That ringing call to holy living is sounded again and again through the epistle.

Now how is a person to live the holy life in a world full of error and sin? Emphatically Paul declares it: this calling was not based on something we could ever be by our own works; but God had a purpose, manifested through Jesus Christ, whereby the calling could be fulfilled.

Repeatedly in Paul's writing, he uses expressions similar to this, about God's purpose in Christ, hidden in past ages, but now made manifest. (See, for example, Romans 16:25-26; 1 Corinthians 2:7-10; Ephesians 1:9-11; 3:3-6;

Colossians 1:26-29; Titus 1:2-3.)

It is not the secret election of certain individuals to eternal life and others to eternal death, which is now made manifest in Christ Jesus. It is, rather, God's eternal purpose to save believers through Jesus Christ. In His manifestation He demonstrated the "life and immortality" which are available to believers through faith in the Lord Jesus Christ.

None of these passages, then, teaches the unconditional election of some to life and others to death, as the Calvinists claim.

To summarize, the Arminian position, with which Wesleyans fully agree, is that election is only in Christ. The Church as the Body of Christ—a corporately-elected people—is assured of eternal victory. Individuals are conditionally elected in Christ, when by repentance and faith they partake of His salvation. Their election is assured as they maintain their faith in Him.

Endnotes

1. *Institutes*, III:xxi:7.

2. *Ibid.*, III:xxi:5.

3. *Ibid.* III:xxi:1, 2.

4. *Ibid.*, I:vi:2.

5. Charles Hodge, *Commentary on the Epistle to the Romans* (New York: Hodder and Stoughton, 1882), p. 459.

6. Robert Shank, *Elect in the Son* (Springfield, MO: Westcott Publishers, 1970), p. 45. His sources are all documented.

7. Forster, Roger T., and Marston, V. Paul, *God's Strategy in Human History* (Wheaton, IL: Tyndale House Publishers, Inc., 1973), p. 136.

8. Arminius, *Op. cit.*, III, p. 354.

9. *Institutes*, III:xxii:3.

10. *Ibid.*, III:xxii:7.

11. Forster and Marston, *Op. cit.*, p. 148.

12. William Barclay, *The Letters of Timothy, Titus, and Philemon* (Edinburgh: The Saint Andrew Press, 1960), p. 168.

5

The Atonement

SHARPLY CONFLICTING VIEWS OF the atonement through Jesus Christ are maintained by Calvinists and Arminians. In fact there are conflicts among Calvinists, many dissenting in some measure from the theory generally identified as Calvinistic.

The Satisfaction Theory
Strong Calvinistic Position

We have earlier traced the logic of Augustine, whereby he proceeded from his premise of the total depravity of man to his view of the atonement. It is by the sovereign and irresistible act of God's will that certain elected individuals are turned to receive salvation, while all others are passed by and left in their sins. This being true, he reasoned, Jesus did not die for all men, but only for those who were predestined to be saved. The atonement was thus limited and efficacious only for the elect.

From this beginning there was a gradual development of the satisfaction theory, which must of necessity harmonize with other tenets of the Reformed, or Calvinistic, faith. It may be summarized under the following points:

1. Sin has an intrinsic demerit or loathsomeness, which makes it totally abhorrent to God and antagonistic to His holiness.

2. Sin must therefore be punished. God's absolute justice requires it. Penalty could not be remitted without a serious violation of His justice, which God will never allow. The Calvinist writer Charles Hodge asserted, "Justice is a form of moral excellence. It belongs to the nature of God. It demands the punishment of sin. If sin be pardoned, it can be pardoned in consistency with the divine justice only on the ground of forensic penal satisfaction."[1]

3. Jesus Christ was ordained to be the substitute for the elect, in two different ways. First, He is the substitute in penalty, taking the guilt of sins upon Himself and receiving punishment equivalent in value to that which was due to all the

elect. Only by such a substitution can the justice of God be satisfied and the elect sinners still be delivered from that death which is the merit of their sins. Christ did not, however, assume the demerit of sin. Demerit and guilt are held to be separable, so that whereas the sinner retains the demerit of sin, Christ took the guilt.

Hodge expressed the position thus:

> If punishment means evil inflicted on the ground of personal demerit, then it is a contradiction to say that the innocent can be punished. But if guilt expresses only the relation of sin to justice and is the obligation under which the sinner is placed to satisfy its demands [the satisfactionist view], then there is nothing in the nature of God as revealed either in his providence or in his word, which forbids the idea that this obligation may on adequate grounds be transferred from one to another, or assumed by one in the place of others.[2]

Here Hodge declares that guilt and punishment are inseparably attached to sin but not to the sinner. Thus, Jesus bore the guilt of sins which we, but not He, committed.

Second, He is the substitute in obedience. No sinner could fulfill the requirements of the law, so Christ perfectly obeyed as a substitute for the elect. Thus it is assured that all guilt—past, present, and future—is borne by Christ, and that His righteousness is placed to the account of those who are predestined unto eternal life.

4. To repeat what was earlier stated, the atonement of Christ is limited in its extent to the salvation of the elect.

We quote Hodge again:

> If God from eternity determined to save one portion of the human race and not another, it seems to be a contradiction to say that the plan of salvation had equal reference to both portions…
>
> Every assertion, therefore, that Christ died for a people, is a denial of the doctrine that He died equally for all men.[3]

This theory is called "the satisfaction theory" because Jesus Christ has fully satisfied the demands of divine justice and righteousness on behalf of those who are ordained to eternal life.

Mild Calvinist Position

The more moderate Calvinistic position has been modified to allow a genuine offer of salvation to all men. Not all persons who might be included in this theological position would agree in all details; but the generally-accepted position may be summarized in the following way.

1. Sin has intrinsic demerit. This tenet is the same as for strong Calvinism.

2. Sin must be punished, because of the justice of God. J. Dwight Pentecost, a representative of this position, has written,

> It is a well-known principle, revealed throughout the Word of God, that a holy and a righteous God must execute the sentence which He had decreed upon sin…
>
> This doctrine presents us the great truth of Scripture that God was faithful to Himself, and to His character, and to His Word to punish the sinner. But punishment on the sinner took place in the Person of a substitute, so that God's judgment was meted out upon One who took our place. God, therefore, can receive the one who does no more than believe, because his sin was borne by a Substitute and his indebtedness was paid by another.[4]

3. Jesus died as a substitute in penalty for all who shall believe on Him for their salvation. This is an important departure from strong Calvinism, in that salvation is freely and sincerely offered to all men. The destiny of men depends upon their response to the call of the Gospel.

Lewis Sperry Chafer wrote from this theological perspective about Christ,

> He died as a substitute for some one else, and that some one else is each and every individual in all the lost world of mankind…
>
> It is something accomplished for every person and in such perfection as to be fully satisfying to the infinite God… It must be believed that the death of Christ has already provided a great potential and provisional value for every guilty sinner, which is now awaiting his personal recognition.
>
> …The ransom price has been paid for all; yet for the one who believes, there is a further work of redemption which is manifested in the transforming and sanctifying power of the Spirit.
>
> Happy is the individual who believes what God has written, and rests in the redeeming work of Christ as his only deliverance from the hopeless estate of the lost.[5]

4. Although sinners are free to accept or reject God's offer of salvation, once they have accepted it, they are eternally secure. Christ is their substitute in penalty for past, present and future sins. He is also their substitute in obedience. Consequently, no sin of theirs shall ever separate them from God. This point will be enlarged in Chapter Seven.

Objections to the Satisfaction Theory

There are numerous and serious objections to the satisfaction theory, which, because of limited space, can only be briefly reviewed here. Arminian authors have forcefully presented these objections in detail.[6]

The Separation of Demerit and Guilt

The Calvinistic position states that, although demerit remains with the sinner, guilt is placed upon Christ. Arminians strongly deny such a possibility, affirming that the guilt and demerit of sin are inseparable. Guilt is not an entity in itself which can be shifted from one person to another. It is, rather, the liability of the sinner to punishment because of the demerit of his sins. Guilt can never be separated from the sin which caused it. Therefore, Christ must either have taken our actual sins, with their demerit, upon Himself, or He did not bear our guilt. It is admitted even by Calvinists that He did not assume any demerit by bearing our sins; hence, it is conclusive that He did not bear our guilt. As Miley has said,

> There can be no more guilt apart from sin than there can be extension without either substance or space. It is not in itself punishable, but simply the punitive amenability of sin to justice. It cannot, therefore, be so put upon Christ as to render him punishable, unless the very sin is put upon him. But this is conceded to be impossible.[7]

It is the intrinsic demerit of sin which makes the sinner liable to penalty, and that very liability is what is meant by guilt. The Calvinistic position asserts that the sinner is entirely freed from penalty, past, present and future, irrespective of any further sin which he may commit. Both guilt and penalty were assumed by Christ in His atoning death on the cross. Now if this be true, we have the strange condition of sinners continuing to incur the demerit of sin, but having no guilt associated with that demerit. Since Christ once for all assumed that guilt for him, the sinner no longer bears it.

If the foregoing position were true, we would be forced to conclude that Christ died, not to transform the sinner, but to transform sin; He does not remove sin from the sinner, but rather removes guilt from sin, so that sin is no longer dangerous. Richard Taylor has explained the objection this way:

> An effect is something which necessarily and intrinsically follows that cause… Sin is the cause; death is the result… "The soul that sinneth, it shall die" (Ezekiel 18:4)… "For the wages of sin is death" (Romans 6:23)… But the Calvinist… does not believe in complete deliverance from all sin. In fact, in his doctrine he holds that one may have even awful sin in the life, but if he has at one time been genuinely regenerated, such sin will not produce the usual effect, eternal death. Therefore Calvinism must involve the premise that the atonement applied in conversion changes the nature of sin.[8]

The plain teaching of the Scriptures is exactly the opposite of this. Jesus came, not to save sin from guilt, but to "save His people from their sins" (Matthew 1:21). Even in the full realization of Christ's atoning merits, sin—all sin—still remains damning. "Sin, when it is finished, bringeth forth death" (James 1:15). "The fearful and unbelieving, and the abominable, and murderers, and whoremongers, and sorcerers, and idolaters, and all liars, shall have their part in the lake which burneth with fire and brimstone: which is the second death" (Revelation 21:8). We may notice that the latter passage speaks of "all liars"; there is no distinction between Christian and non-Christian liars—or murderers, or unbelievers.

The Invalidation of Forgiveness

If it is true, as the satisfactionists assert, that Jesus on the cross took away all guilt and penalty from elect sinners, it must necessarily follow that such sinners no longer incur guilt for their sins, and therefore need no forgiveness. Hodge has said,

> If the claims of justice are satisfied, they cannot be again enforced. This is the analogy between the work of Christ and the payment of a debt... In both cases the persons for whom the satisfaction is made are certainly freed. Their exemption or deliverance is in both cases, and equally in both, a matter of justice.[9]

Now we know that at the time when a debt is paid, the debtor is immediately released from all obligation connected with that debt. According to the analogy which Hodge presented, then, since Christ did pay the elect sinner's debt on the cross, the sinner has no further obligation for sin. He is no longer guilty. Dr. Symington in his *Atonement and Intercession* wrote,

> The death of Christ being a legal satisfaction for sin, all for whom he died must enjoy the remission of their offenses. It is as much at variance with strict justice or equity that any for whom Christ has given satisfaction should continue under condemnation, as that they should have been delivered from guilt without any satisfaction being given for them at all.[10]

Such teaching again is contrary to the Word of God and the work of the Spirit in the hearts of sinners. The Bible teaches that the entire world is guilty before God's law, and every individual shares in that guilt until he comes to Christ to be justified (free of guilt) by faith. (See Romans 3:19-26 and 1 Corinthians 11:27-32, for example.) It is the work of the Holy Spirit to "reprove the world of sin" (John 16:8). A multitude of Christians can testify that the Spirit's reproving work produced in them such a painful sense of their guilt that they gladly repented and sought God's mercy by faith in Jesus Christ. If such guilt is real, it follows that

Jesus' death did not immediately remove it.

Referring once more to the analogy of a debt, we may observe that when a debt is paid, it is not forgiven. In Matthew 18:23-25, Jesus told of a king who had a servant with a huge debt. At first the king demanded payment, but later had compassion "and forgave him the debt." Now that forgiveness meant that the debt did not have to be paid. There are two mutually exclusive solutions of a debt: it may be forgiven or it must be paid; both conditions cannot apply to the same debt.

The same conditions apply precisely to the forgiveness of sins. If sin is forgiven, then it is not punished; if it is punished, then it is not forgiven. According to the satisfactionist position, though, every sin must be punished because of the unalterable demand of God's justice. Jesus took the punishment in full for the elect; the non-elect must endure their own punishment. The system logically leaves no proper place for present forgiveness. Guilt might cease to exist in such a system, just as a debt ceases to exist when it is paid, but it would not be forgiven.

Scriptures are so abundant concerning God's forgiveness of sins that quotations are unnecessary. They firmly establish the conclusion that Jesus was not punished for our sins. It is true that He provided the basis for forgiveness and the way in which He did it we shall see in our study of the governmental theory of the atonement.

A Limited Atonement

There is no area in which the contrast between Calvinism and Arminianism is any more definite than in consideration of the extent of the atonement. Calvinists have insisted that Christ in His death provided atonement only for the elect, as has already been illustrated. Arminius strongly opposed such a view and insisted that the atonement was provided for all men.

There are a number of good reasons for opposing the doctrine of a limited atonement. First, it impugns the sincere purpose of God in providing an atonement. If God had been acting only from His absolute sovereignty, He need not have offered His Son as a sacrifice; He could simply have forgiven whom He chose, with regard for nothing aside from His own volition. God did offer His Son, however, and it is certain that He had adequate purpose for doing so. As we shall soon see, part of that purpose lay in maintaining the integrity and honor of His government. In addition, the gift of His Son was a manifestation of His love toward lost men and the price He was willing to pay to redeem them. "For God so loved the world, that he gave his only begotten Son, that whosoever believeth in him should not perish, but have everlasting life" (John 3:16).

Now the question arises, what part of the world did God love: just the elect, or all men? All men by nature stood in exactly the same relation to Him. He created them all, and all fell in Adam. "There is no difference: for all have sinned, and come short of the glory of God" (Romans 3:22, 23). If God really loved fallen, sinful men enough to give His Son, and if all men were naturally in the same relation to Him, how could He be consistent and arbitrarily withhold the benefits of that love from some while bestowing it on others? Yet A. W. Pink, writing from a strong Calvinist position, declared, "The fact is, that the love of God is a truth for the saints only, and to present it to the enemies of God is to take the children's bread and cast it to the dogs."[11]

Arminians insist that God loved the whole world. What He desired for one fallen sinner, He desired for all, for all were by nature exactly alike before Him.

A second consideration is in the forceful and unmistakable statements of the Scriptures. Only a few can be cited, with some others noted for reference.[12] "As I live, saith the Lord God, I have no pleasure in the death of the wicked; but that the wicked turn from his way and live" (Ezekiel 33:11). "God our Savior… will have all men to be saved, and to come unto the knowledge of the truth. For there is one God, and one mediator between God and men, the man Christ Jesus; who gave himself a ransom for all, to be testified in due time" (1 Timothy 2:3-6). "But we see Jesus, who was made a little lower than the angels for the suffering of death, crowned with glory and honor; that he by the grace of God should taste death for every man" (Hebrews 2:9). "The Lord is not slack concerning his promise, as some count slackness; but is longsuffering to usward, not willing that any should perish, but that all should come to repentance" (2 Peter 3:9). If there can be any clear meaning whatsoever to the foregoing verses, it is that God desires the salvation of all men and that He has made adequate provision so that all might be saved if they will.

One more verse may be given: "For therefore we both labor and suffer reproach, because we trust in the living God, who is the Savior of all men, specially of those that believe" (1 Timothy 4:10). In the Calvinist view of the irresistible will of God, if God truly should will the salvation of all men, then all must surely be saved; otherwise, God is not truly sovereign. But the foregoing verse shows the distinction between what is possible and what is actual in God's saving work. He has provided salvation as a real possibility for all men. In that sense, He is "the Savior of all men." But salvation can become actual only as the individual responds in faith to the call of the gospel. So, in a special sense, Christ is the Savior to believers only. In perfect agreement with the Scriptures, Arminians believe in a universal atonement provided for all men. Yet they are not universalists: they do not believe that all men actually will be saved just because God made provisions for all.

A third objection to limited atonement lies in the great commission which Christ gave to His church. "And he said unto them, Go ye into all the world, and preach the gospel to every creature. He that believeth and is baptized shall be saved; but he that believeth not shall be damned" (Mark 16:15, 16). How could any gospel preacher sincerely go forth to call all men to repentance when he believes that God has irrevocably predestined at least half of them to eternal damnation and made repentance impossible for them? How could he honestly offer salvation to all, when he believes that it is not provided for all? How could he fervently persuade men to believe, when faith is given or withheld according to the sovereign decree of God and nothing else? It is because of questions like these that a great many people with evangelistic passion have turned away from the idea of a limited atonement and have sincerely offered salvation to all men, upon the simple conditions of repentance and faith.

The Governmental Theory

Hugo Grotius, the brilliant legal expert and initiator of the modern principles of international law, was a supporter of Arminius. He advocated the governmental theory of the atonement as being true to the Scriptures and the moral responsibility of men. The principal points of his theory, as it is now generally accepted by Arminians, are as follows:

1. God is the supreme ruler in a moral universe and is therefore responsible for maintaining the honor and integrity of His government over that universe. Such a responsibility has a two-fold aspect. First, He must consistently enforce the holy principles of government and manifest justice toward all who violate His laws. Second, He must be always concerned for the welfare of His creatures, protecting their interests and promoting virtue among them. Punishment is administered not only because of the guilt of the sinner, though that is the primary reason; it also has a restraining influence upon all observers, reminding them of the danger of sin and encouraging them toward virtue. For God to withhold

punishment from the sinner would be to remove the restraining influence upon others, unless some substitute for punishment is introduced which will likewise demonstrate the holiness of God and the horror of sin.

2. Sin, because of its extreme demerit, deserves eternal penalty. Therefore, in the exercise of His justice, God must either punish sin with such eternal penalty or provide a substitute for punishment, which will equally maintain both the integrity of His government and the welfare of His creatures.

Here appears the critical difference between the satisfaction and governmental theories. The former declares that all sin must be punished, while the latter asserts that punishment may be withheld and sin forgiven if a proper substitute for penalty is introduced.

3. The motivating cause of redemption is God's love. While in His justice God fully recognizes sin as meriting punishment, in His love He desires to save men from punishment, if He can at the same time uphold the honor of His government and the welfare of His creatures. This He has fully done in the atoning death of Jesus Christ. The punishment of sin is thus not an absolute requirement of divine justice. Because of the atonement, sin may be forgiven; and, as we have already shown, if it is forgiven, it is not punished. St. Paul declared that through the redemption in Christ Jesus, God has manifested His righteousness, "that he might be just, and the justifier of him which believeth in Jesus" (Romans 3:26). To justify is to declare free from guilt and punishment. God is right in doing so because of the atonement.

4. The death of Christ was not a punishment for sins, as the satisfactionists assert, but rather a substitute for punishment. The Scriptures never assert that Jesus took our guilt upon Himself, or that He was punished for our sins. Instead, we are often told that Christ *suffered* for our sins. For example, we read in 1 Peter 3:18, "For Christ also hath once suffered for sins, the just for the unjust, that he might bring us to God, being put to death in the flesh, but quickened by the Spirit."

This is not in the least to belittle the suffering of Christ on the cross. In his prophecy Isaiah, for the first time, clearly identified the Messiah as the Lamb of God. He declared (Isaiah 53:5, 10-11), "He was wounded for our transgressions, he was bruised for our iniquities: the chastisement of our peace was upon him; and with his stripes we are healed... It pleased the Lord to bruise him; he hath put him to grief: when thou shalt make his soul an offering for sin,... the pleasure of the Lord shall prosper in his hand. He shall see of the travail of his soul, and shall be satisfied."

There was surely a divine "satisfaction" in the death of Christ; it made possible the redemption of all mankind, especially of those who believe. He fully bore the sins of the world. But He did this as an "offering for sin," as Isaiah said. Priests pronounced over the heads of the animal offerings the sins of the people; but there was no thought that those animals were being punished. They were suffering and they were dying, that the human sinners might not have to suffer and die for those sins.

If Jesus had truly borne the full punishment for sins, He would have had to die eternally, for that was part of the penalty. This He did not do, although "He tasted death for every man." Yet He suffered enough to satisfy equally well the demands of God's justice, so that we might be freed from sin's penalty.

Second Corinthians 5:21 is frequently employed by Calvinists in their effort to prove that Jesus actually assumed the guilt of our sins. Some have pressed the meaning of the verse farther and asserted that He became a sinner in behalf of all the elect. The verse says, "For he hath made him to be sin for us, who knew no sin; that we might be made the righteousness of God in him."

The common Arminian understanding is that Jesus was made a *sin offering* for us. Ralston explained:

> The sense evidently is, that Christ was made a sin-offering, as a *substitute for us.* In no other sense can it be said that he "was made *sin*." The word *amartian*, here rendered sin, is by Macnight and others translated *sin-offering*. So it is frequently used in the Septuagint... So also it is used in Hebrews 13:11: "For the bodies of those beasts, whose blood is brought into the sanctuary by the high-priest for (*amartias*) a *sin-offering*." Now, it is clear, that the blood of beasts was offered "for sin" in no other sense than that of an expiation or atonement. Hence, we perceive that Christ was "made sin for us" in no other sense than that of a vicarious offering.[13]

The distinction between suffering and punishment is of real significance. As we have earlier seen, if Jesus was punished for any man's sins, then that man can never be punished for his own sins, for no sin can justly be punished twice. Further, if Jesus was punished for our sins, then forgiveness is meaningless. Sins may be either punished or forgiven, but not both. If, as we assert, Jesus suffered as a substitute for punishment, then sinners, upon the basis of repentance and faith in Jesus Christ, may be forgiven of their sins. If, on the contrary, they refuse the substitute provided for them, they still merit punishment for all their sins, including that very sin of refusing the salvation provided through Jesus Christ.

5. The suffering of Christ as a substitute for our punishment fully upholds the honor of divine government and exhibits the awful costliness of sin, while still providing a way whereby God can display His love in the pardon of penitent sinners.

We may all look upon the wondrous atonement and declare with St. Paul that God is just while He justifies those who believe on Jesus!

6. Because of the substitutionary death of Christ, God now sincerely offers salvation to all men, as the Scriptures abundantly attest. Salvation is conditional, however, and only those who repent and believe on Jesus Christ will be saved. The atonement is unlimited, though its effects are limited, not by the sovereign will of God, but by the impenitence and unbelief of men.

Human responsibility in responding to the offer of mercy will be examined in the next chapter.

Endnotes

1. Hodge, *Op. cit.*, Vol. II, p. 488.

2. *Ibid.*, p. 532.

3. *Ibid.*, pp. 548-49.

4. Pentecost, *Op. cit.*, p. 51.

5. Lewis Sperry Chafer, *Salvation* (Grand Rapids, MI: Zondervan Publishing House, 1917), pp. 32, 33, 38.

6. See for example, John Miley, *Atonement in Christ* (New York: Phillips and Hunt, 1880), pp. 150-187.

7. John Miley, *Systematic Theology* (New York: Eaton and Mains, 1894), Vol. II, p. 147.

8. Richard S. Taylor, *A Right Conception of Sin* (Kansas City, MO: Beacon Hill Press, 1945), pp. 22-23.

9. Hodge, *Op. cit.*, p. 472.

10. William Symington, *The Atonement and Intercession of Christ* (New York: Robert Carter and Brothers, 1858), p. 190.

11. Pink, *Op. cit.*, p. 246.

12. Other examples are Isaiah 45:22; Isaiah 55:1; Ezekiel 18:32; Matthew 11:28; 22:9; John 7:37; Romans 10:12; and Revelation 22:17.

13. Thomas N. Ralston, *Elements of Divinity* (Salem, OH: Convention Book Store, 1971 reprint), pp. 226-27.

6

The Way of Salvation

THE VARIOUS THEOLOGICAL POSITIONS under consideration agree on the fact that God has ordained a wondrous plan of salvation. They differ significantly, however, with respect to the role which individual persons play in that salvation. We must, therefore, consider the divine and human responsibilities in human salvation. Is it altogether the working of God upon passive sinners, or is the sinner in some measure to participate in assuring his own salvation? If a person must assume some responsibility, can we still say that salvation is altogether of grace, or must we conclude that it is partly by works? These are serious questions, and the answers differ according to the doctrinal positions under study.

The Classical Calvinist Position

Chapter 1 included reference to the five-point summary of Calvinism which became a standard doctrinal statement in the Seventeenth Century and has been used ever since as a concise summary. It may be stated thus:

1) Total depravity, by which sinners are naturally unable to do anything toward their own salvation;

2) Unconditional election, or particular predestination, by which each person is divinely chosen either to eternal life or eternal damnation;

3) Limited atonement, providing for the salvation only of those who are elected to eternal life;

4) Irresistible grace or effectual calling, by which it is assured absolutely that those who are elected shall be saved; and

5) Perseverance to the end, or unconditional security, by which it is assured that those who once savingly believe on Christ shall be eternally preserved from falling away and being lost.[1]

Our present chapter involves primarily the first and fourth points, total depravity and irresistible grace. We have already observed Augustine's reaction to Pelagius, whereby he held that mankind has been so thoroughly depraved through the fall of Adam that he is entirely incapable of any response to grace. Commenting on Ezekiel 36:26-27 ("I will take away the stony heart out of your flesh, and I will give you an heart of flesh...") Calvin wrote,

> If there is any softness in a stone; if you can make it tender, and flexible into any shape, then it may be said, that the human heart may be shaped for rectitude, provided that which is imperfect in it is supplemented by divine grace. But if the Spirit, by the above similitude, meant to show that no good thing can ever be extracted from our heart until it is made altogether new, let us not attempt to share with Him what He claims for himself alone. If it is like turning a stone into flesh when God turns us to the study of rectitude, everything proper to our own will is abolished, . . . I also say, that it is created anew, not because the will then begins to exist, but because it is turned from evil to good.[2]

With this assumption as background, the entire work of salvation is viewed as due to God's sovereign grace, which is entirely irresistible. God applies His superior will to the finite will of elected sinners and moves them effectively along the pathway to eternal salvation.

Such a view is known as "monergism," the operation of only one source of energy in effecting human salvation. God alone is responsible, and those whom He elects will be eternally saved without exception.

Order of Events in Salvation

The fourth point of Calvinism concerns irresistible grace or effectual calling. Under this heading it is proper to consider the order of events in the salvation of the soul. Williamson, explaining the *Westminster Confession of Faith*, writes thus:

> We here begin a survey of the *ordo salutis*—the order of the application of redemption to the elect. In this order we distinguish the following: (1) the free offer of salvation in the gospel (God's general *call*), (2) *regeneration* (the creative act of God making the elect new beings in heart), (3) *conversion* (the exercise of that new heart in responding to the gospel in repentance and faith), (4) *justification* (the judicial act of God upon repentance and faith by which he declares and constitutes his elect "just" or righteous, (5) *adoption* (the act by which God admits them into the rights and privileges of sons of God, (6) *sanctification* (the work of God's Spirit by which the elect are enabled to persevere in faith unto ever greater conformity to the will of God), and (7) *glorification* (by which, at the resurrection of the body, the believer is at last constituted perfect in Christ both in body and soul, forever).[3]

First, there is the *calling of God*. Calvinists distinguish between the general and the effectual calling. By the general call the gospel is to be preached with sincerity to all mankind. We cannot know who are the elect of God, so in order to reach them, we are to preach to all people God's message of salvation. The calling will be effectual, though, only to the elect, since none other will have the grace imparted by which he may respond to the gospel invitation. The general call saves nobody, but it may be a basis for condemnation upon those who refuse it. The unregenerated will of sinners always rejects the call, and they are thus rendered worthy of the severest judgment.

To the elect the calling is made effectual by the Holy Spirit. The *Westminster Confession* declares,

> This effectual call is of God's free and special grace alone, not from any thing at all foreseen in man; who is altogether passive therein, until, being quickened and renewed by the Holy Spirit, he is thereby enabled to answer this call, and to embrace the grace offered and conveyed in it.[4]

Regeneration is alluded to in the foregoing paragraph as that quickening and renewing by the Holy Spirit which enables a sinner to answer the call. It may be observed that, in this interpretation, regeneration is entirely a divine act wrought upon a dead soul, without any participation by the sinner whatever. Faith does not precede regeneration but rather follows after it. By this divine act the sinner is made spiritually alive; he is born from above. No repentance, restitution, or conversion is necessary for regeneration; it is produced by the sovereign power of God alone. Although the matter will be discussed in detail later, it is well to add here that the imparted divine life that regenerates is guaranteed to remain eternally. There are no conditions whatever on the part of the sinner in the change from condemnation to eternal salvation. All is of God's grace.

Conversion is the response of the regenerated person in which he exercises faith and repentance. Notice the order here: first, regeneration; then faith and repentance, the latter two of which are comprehended in conversion. Williamson comments,

> To begin with, we must observe that regeneration is inseparable from its effects. One of the effects is faith. Another is repentance. Regeneration is the renewing of the heart or mind, and the renewed personality must and will act according to its nature. In faith and repentance we simply see the new nature beginning to assert itself.[5]

One reason why Calvinists so strongly insist that repentance and faith follow regeneration is their belief that such repentance and faith are human works, and if they were conditions of the new birth, then we would no longer be saved by grace alone, but would have to give part of the credit for salvation to human works. Pentecost said,

> Repentance is not a prerequisite to salvation; for if repentance is required, salvation is based, at least in part, upon works... We would suggest to you from the Word of God that repentance is included in believing. It is not a separate act which conditions salvation, but rather it is included in the act of believing..."[6]

As we shall later see, the Arminians strongly disagree with this interpretation.

Justification follows regeneration and conversion. Faith, which is bestowed as a gift of God and is dependent on the human will only insofar as the will is irresistibly moved by the Spirit of God, brings justification. For the Calvinist, justification means that the righteousness of Christ is imputed to the sinner, so that even if he continues to sin, God counts him as being righteous. This is because of the effects of Christ's substitution in both penalty and obedience. Because He took the sinner's penalty, the sinner is no longer counted guilty of any sins, past, present or future. Because Christ was the sinner's substitute in obedience, God counts the sinner as righteous, even though he often in fact disobeys God's law. Calvin stated the matter thus:

> We must strongly insist on these two things: That no believer ever performed one work which, if tested by the strict judgment of God, could escape condemnation; and, moreover, that were this granted to be possible (though it is not), yet the act being vitiated and polluted by the sins of which it is certain that the author of it is guilty, it is deprived of its merit. This is the cardinal point of the present discussion . . . . Christ ever remains a Mediator to reconcile the Father to us, and there is a perpetual efficacy in his death—*viz.* ablution, satisfaction, expiation; in short, perfect obedience, by which all our iniquities are covered...
>
> The Father embraces us in Christ when he clothes us with the innocence of Christ, and accepts it as ours, so that in consideration of it he regards us as holy, pure, and innocent. For the righteousness of Christ (as it alone is perfect, so it alone can stand the scrutiny of God) must appear in court for us, and as a surety represent us judicially. Provided with this righteousness, we constantly obtain the remission of sins through faith. Our imperfection and impurity, covered with this purity, are not imputed, but are as it were buried, so as not to come under judgment until the hour arrive when the old man being destroyed, and plainly extinguished in us, the divine goodness shall receive us into beatific peace with the new Adam, there to await the day of the Lord, on which, being clothed with incorruptible bodies, we shall be translated to the glory of the heavenly kingdom.[7]

A distinction is thus made between the believer's *state* and his *standing*. The state refers to what he is in fact, still a sinner, whereas the standing refers to how God sees or considers him, as pure and perfect in Christ Jesus.

Adoption is the act of God, accompanying justification, by which the believer becomes a son of God, and is entitled to be an heir of God and a joint-heir with Christ. Arminians have no difficulty with the Calvinist at this point, except that the former hold it possible to lose one's place as a son through willful sin and rebellion, while the latter disallow the possibility.

Sanctification is viewed as merely a process whereby the believer, appropriating the Word of God and the power of the Spirit, more and more gains victory in the struggle with fleshly lusts. Yet it is never to be complete in this life. Growth in grace and holiness must continue to the end, the goal always being beyond us.

Glorification must await the coming day of resurrection, when we shall be like Christ and shall see Him as He is. Calvinists hold that sin must adhere to every believer until death and that only in the glorified state will we be morally complete. Wesleyans agree that glorification brings the final freedom from the faulty and frail body, but they insist that indwelling sin may be removed during the present life, whereas infirmities cling to the moral constitution until we are glorified. The Bible is consistent in its distinction between sin and infirmity.

The Wesleyan-Arminian Position

In this chapter the mild Calvinistic position is reserved to last place, because it will be more easily understood as a position between the other two.

The Nature of Faith

While we will consider the order of events in salvation, it will be helpful first to examine the Arminian (and we believe biblical) concept of faith, because here the sharp contrast between the systems comes into focus.

First, faith is a requisite condition for justification, yet is not a meritorious work. Wesley wrote,

> We cannot, therefore, be justified by our works; because this would be, to be justified by some merit of our own . . . .
>
> The life and death of our Lord is the sole meritorious cause of this mercy, which must be firmly believed and trusted in by us. Our faith therefore in him, though not more meritorious than any of our actions, yet has a nearer relation to the promises of pardon through him, and is the means and instrument whereby we embrace and receive them.[8]

Adam Clarke, the Methodist commentator contemporary with Wesley, wrote in reference to Ephesians 2:8-9 ("For by grace are ye saved through faith; and that not of yourselves: it is the gift of God: not of works, lest any man should boast"),

> But whether are we to understand, faith or salvation as being the gift of God? This question is answered by the Greek text: ... The relative *touto* [that], which is the neuter gender, cannot stand for *pistis*, *faith*, which is feminine; but it has the whole sentence that goes before for its antecedent. But it may be asked: Is not faith the gift of God? Yes, as to the grace by which it is produced; but the grace or power to believe, and the act of believing, are two different things. Without the grace or power to believe no man ever did or can believe; but with that power the act of faith is a man's own. God never believes for any man, no more than he repents for him; the penitent, through this grace enabling him, believes for himself: nor does he believe necessarily, or impulsively when he has the power; the power to believe may be present long before it is exercised.[9]

Clarke summarized well the Wesleyan position: faith is exercised with the enablement of the Spirit of God, in such a way that, although it involves the human will, there is no merit in the act, so it can be said without reservation that we are saved by grace and not by works. When Jesus commanded, "Lazarus, come forth" (John 11:43), Lazarus responded voluntarily and participated in the remarkable event; yet it could not properly be said that the resurrection was of human works. When a person is offered a gift large enough to pay all of his debts, and he stretches out his hand to receive it, there is a voluntary response in receiving the gift; yet surely there is no merit in extending the hand. The merit is entirely with the giver. So it is in our salvation. Faith is our response to the divine offer of salvation; and while it involves the human will, enabled by the Spirit of God, there is no merit whatever in the response. Salvation is still all of grace, through faith.

This position is identified by the term "synergism," because two sources of action are cooperating together, the divine and the human. It stands in contrast with Calvinistic "monergism," which attributes all the action to God alone.

Second, all of the human ability to respond in faith to the call of God is divinely provided through the Holy Spirit, so that there is no ground whatever for boasting as if individuals were capable of saving themselves. It is at this point where Calvinists often misrepresent Arminians, as if they boasted in human ability and works. Unfortunately, some Arminians of a very liberal persuasion have given cause for the charge, but Wesleyan-Arminians consistently hold that salvation is entirely of grace and not of human good works.

The special grace of God which precedes salvation, enabling sinners to respond in faith to the call of God is called "preventing" [preceding] or "prevenient" grace. While the term is not taken from Scriptures, it has been consistently used as expressing a biblical truth. William Pope has well summarized the Wesleyan position:

> The Holy Ghost is here the Author of preliminary grace: that is, the kind of preparatory influence which is imparted outside of the temple of Christ's mystical body, or rather in the outer court of that temple... It must be remembered that it is *the Grace of the Lord Jesus Christ* flowing from and revealing the *Love of God* that is dispensed even to the outer world in *the Communion* of the Holy Ghost. But it must be remembered that this prevenient influence is literally bound up with the human use of it, being without meaning apart from that use; and, moreover, that of itself it is not saving, though it is unto salvation.[10]

Numerous passages of scripture may be summoned to demonstrate this "prevenient grace." Philippians 2:13 declares, "Remember it is God who, in kindness, is at work within you, enabling you both to will and to work" (20th Century N.T.). God does not do the willing for us, but He enables us to will and to do. We could neither will nor do what is pleasing to God unless we were divinely enabled. As Jesus said, "Without me ye can do nothing" (John 15:5). Yet it is also true, as Paul asserted, "I can do all things through Christ which strengtheneth me" (Philippians 4:13).

Another verse which speaks of prevenient grace is Titus 2:11, "For the grace of God that bringeth salvation hath appeared to all men." The word "appeared" often refers to the shining forth of a heavenly body, such as the sun. Just as the sun does not reach all parts of the earth at one and the same instant, so the grace of God through preaching does not reach all parts simultaneously. However, it is designed to reach all parts, and it is God's often-repeated purpose that the gospel is to be preached in all the world for a witness to every creature. By the preaching of this gospel, all men are drawn unto Jesus Christ (John 12;32). Without this drawing, which is initiated by the Father, no man can come unto Jesus Christ for salvation (John 6:44); with it any person is enabled to come if he will. Even in the absence of preaching, there is the grace of conscience, of which St. Paul speaks in Romans 2:14-15, and natural revelation , mentioned in Romans 1:18-20.

The Calvinists speak of "common grace," which is similar to prevenient grace, in that it is directed toward all men, and in that it brings wholesome influences to all, such as the restraint of conscience. According to the Calvinists, however, it is not sufficient to bring sinners to repentance. The effectual calling is necessary for that and is accompanied by irresistible grace unto salvation for the elect only.

Third, Wesleyans hold that faith is dynamic and that it must be constantly exercised until the very end of human probation. Wynkoop has observed,

> "Believing" is always in the progressive present tense in the Greek, indicating a continuing responsibility on the part of the believer to maintain the new "walk of faith," which includes obedience and love (cf John 1:7; 3:16-17; Acts 13:39; Romans 10:9; John 20:3).[11]

Calvinists virtually rob faith of any moral quality, when they assign it to the sovereign act of God and make one initial act of faith to guarantee an eternal standing of righteousness before God, regardless of the moral state of the individual "believer." In fact, it is a misnomer to call such a person a "believer," when continuing faith is not a real responsibility of the individual and when it has no dynamic moral quality about it. This subject will be explored further in our treatment of the believer's security.

Fourth, evangelical faith has obedience as an essential element. If there is a deliberate disobedience to the will of God, saving faith is impossible. Paul speaks of the obedience of faith (Romans 1:5; 16:26). The two are so closely related that "disobedient" and "unbelieving" are derived from the same Greek root word in the New Testament. It is no more possible to trust Christ in the evangelical sense while disobeying Him than it is to be flying in an airplane toward Asia over the Pacific, and be drawing near to the United States at the same time. They are plainly contradictory conditions. Yet the Calvinists hold that both are possible, since faith is bestowed sovereignly by divine decree once for all, and that it is totally independent of the moral condition of the individual. If, as they say, faith in Christ brings a believer into a standing of perpetual righteousness based entirely on what is imputed from Christ to him, then it is proper to divorce faith from moral character. The Scripture does not do this, though. As we have seen, the New Testament consistently relates faith and obedience. We must then conclude that the Calvinist position is in error.

Order of Events in Salvation

Having observed the strategic differences with regard to faith, we now proceed to examine the order of events as salvation is accomplished for an individual.

As in the Calvinistic system, the first phase is the *gospel call*. The difference lies in the Arminian claim that the call is offered with equal sincerity to all men.

Arminians make no such distinction as that between the general and effectual calls as viewed by Calvinists. There may be a proper distinction between an indirect or universal call and a direct or immediate call. The former is related to the natural revelation of God through His creation and through conscience, whereas the latter relates to the revelation of God through His Word. In either case, God is genuine in His offer of love and salvation, willing not the death of any, but that all shall come to repentance. This fact of the universality of the gospel invitation has been established in our treatment of the atonement and need not be labored further at this point.

When the call of God comes to any sinner through the preaching of the Word, it is accompanied not only by the innate power of the Word, but by the direct operation of the Spirit upon the heart. The Word is the "sword of the Spirit," by which he opens the heart and reveals God's saving truth. This operation of the Spirit brings awakening and conviction, so that sinners are caused to see the danger of their sinful state and the offer of mercy through Jesus Christ. Both the divine action and the effect of the Word are declared in Luke 24:45 and Acts 16:14. "Then opened he their understanding, that they might understand the scriptures." "Whose heart the Lord opened, that she [Lydia] attended unto the things that were spoken of Paul."

It is this illumination of the Word by the Spirit and its application to the human heart, which is called "light" in the Bible. "Whatsoever doth make manifest is light," St. Paul asserts (Ephesians 5:13).

The response to light when it comes to the individual is of the greatest conceivable moment, for on that response depends eternal destiny. The Calvinists allow no element of true human freedom between the effective call of God and regeneration. The Bible places the utmost importance on the individual response to the call, indicating that there is true human freedom and responsibility involved. Because of its vital importance, we must look more in detail at this issue of human response.

A good place to examine it is the story of St. Paul's ministry at Thessalonica. Here is part of the record: "For our gospel came not unto you in word only, but also in power, and in the Holy Ghost, and in much assurance [persuasion, conviction]... And ye became followers of us, and of the Lord, having received (Greek: *dekomai*) the word in much affliction, with joy of the Holy Ghost" (1 Thessalonians 1:5-6). "For this cause also thank we God without ceasing, because, when ye received (Greek: *paralambano*) the word of God which ye heard of us, ye received (Greek: *dekomai*) it not as the word of men, but as it is in truth, the word of God, which effectually worketh also in you that believe" (1 Thessalonians 2:13).

There is a significant distinction in the two words translated "received." Thayer says of *paralambano* that it means to "receive something transmitted... to receive with the mind."[12] Concerning *dekomai* he says, "to receive favorably... embrace, make one's own, approve, not to reject... The suggestion of a welcoming or an appropriating reception generally cleaves to *dekomai*."[13] *Paralambano* then refers to an initial evaluation with the mind, whereas *dekomai* involves a voluntary acceptance of that which is approved with the mind. Commenting on 1 Thessalonians 2:13, quoted above, which includes both words, Whedon has said, "*Received*—by the ear. *Received*—Different Greek word from the former *received*, signifying acceptance by will."[14] The Thessalonians first entertained the Word in their minds, weighing it as to its truthfulness and its claims, then deciding whether to appropriate and live by it or not. As is almost always true, some did and some didn't.

Acts 17 describes the process as it occurred.

> And Paul, as his manner was, went in unto them, and three sabbath days reasoned with them out of the scriptures, opening and alleging, that Christ must needs have suffered, and risen again from the dead; and that this Jesus, whom I preach unto you, is Christ. And some of them believed, and consorted with Paul and Silas; and of the devout Greeks a great multitude, and of the chief women not a few. But the Jews which believed not, moved with envy, took unto them certain lewd fellows of the baser sort, and gathered a company, and set all the city on an uproar..." (2-5).

St. Paul first appealed to their minds with reasoning from the Scriptures. It was not mere logic, however, for there was power and conviction in his message. Notice that those who refused to accept the message were "moved with envy." They weighted the message of God's *truth* against their own *selfish desires*, and chose to follow envy rather than truth. The seriousness of that choice is put in bold form in 2 Thessalonians 2:9-12. Speaking of the antichrist, Paul said,

> whose coming is after the working of Satan with all power and signs and lying wonders, and with all deceivableness of unrighteousness in them that perish; because they received no [Greek: *dekomai*] the love of the truth, that they might be saved. And for this cause God shall send them strong delusion, that they should believe a lie; that they all might be damned who believed not the truth, but had pleasure in unrighteousness.

Notice that the truth came to these people, just as it did to the believers, but they did not love it and follow after it, because as they weighed alternatives, they put *pleasure* above *truth*. As a consequence, by God's decree, they have condemnation rather than salvation.

This is such a serious truth that it is stated repeatedly in the Word of God. When truth is revealed through the Word by the Spirit, it makes demands on people. It is not just novelty or opinion, but divine, eternal truth. Our minds were given to us to discover truth, and our wills to follow after it. But the sinful heart places lust and pleasure over against truth. When a person, in such case, decides against truth, he is essentially asking for error and deception. And God declares that He will allow such people to be deceived, although they will be condemned for the choice they make.

To make God totally responsible for the reprobation of such persons is to charge Him with the lust and selfish pleasure-seeking that moves them against the truth. Arminians will never lay the charge against God, but hold the individuals responsible. God gives them light and conviction of the truth. He gives them the ability to choose and grace enough to follow the truth if they will so choose. But they alone make the choice.

The same serious fact appears in John 3:19, "And this is the condemnation, that light is come into the world, and men loved darkness rather than light, because their deeds were evil." There is the choice on which judgment is based: between light and darkness. Each person makes an evaluation in terms of which he loves more. The Thessalonian unbelievers were condemned because they did not receive (*dekomai*) the love of the truth, that they might be saved.

One more illustration must suffice, though the subject could be expanded much more largely. A rich young ruler came to Jesus inquiring the way to eternal life. Jesus told him to sell his possessions, give to the poor, and come and follow Him, for then he would have treasure in heaven. "But when the young man heard that saying, he went away sorrowful: for he had great possessions" (Matthew 19:22). He weighed the alternatives of eternal versus temporal treasures and chose the latter, though it was painful to make the choice. Jesus evaluated the case as follows: "A rich man shall hardly enter into the kingdom of heaven" (v. 23). Now if eternal life or death is simply a matter of God's sovereign, irresistible action upon the human soul, there is nothing hard about a rich man's entering the kingdom of heaven. God would simply exert the necessary force to overcome the appeal of earthly riches. But the matter is not settled that way. The person makes his own evaluation and the appeal of great, immediate wealth is so powerful that it usually overcomes the appeal of eternal truth and eternal reward. That is how Jesus concluded the matter, and we are wise not to alter His conclusion.

Accompanying the call of God there is *prevenient grace*, which has already been described. It is by this grace that sinners are enabled to respond to the call if they will. When the call is issued, it carries with it the enablement of the Spirit whereby the call can be obeyed. When Jesus said, "Lazarus, come forth," he was enabled to do so, by that divine Word. When God says, "Awake thou that sleepest, and arise from the dead, and Christ shall give thee light" (Ephesians 5:14), there is divine power sufficient to awaken the sinner. He may arise if he will; he may have light if he will receive it. But alas, a great many, though awakened, prefer to go back to sleep in spiritual death rather than to face the light and walk in it. That is their own choice and responsibility. God has by grace awakened them and given them light, but He does not force them to walk in it.

Following the call, there must be *repentance* and *faith* if the sinner is to be saved. The order is important. Calvinists hold that faith comes before repentance, but the biblical order is the opposite, though the two are closely related. Jesus said to the chief priests and elders of the Jews, "John came unto you in the way of righteousness, and ye believed him not: but the publicans and harlots believed him: and ye, when ye had seen it, repented not afterward, that ye might believe him" (Matthew 21:32). Repentance here is plainly given as a condition of believing. In another encounter Jesus told them they could not believe because they would not turn away from their own selfish honor to the truth of God.

> Search the scriptures; for in them ye think ye have eternal life: and they are they which testify of me. And ye will not come to me that ye might have life... How can ye believe, which receive honour one of another, and seek not the honour that cometh from God only? (John 5:39-44).

Speaking of repentance and giving a definition, Wesley said, "Repentance and 'fruits meet for repentance' go before faith... By repentance, I mean conviction of sin, producing real desires and sincere resolutions of amendment."[15] Grider has defined the word "repentance" as follows: "When repentance reaches its real essence... the lost soul undergoes an utter change of mind regarding sin and God. He turns from sin to God with purpose to obey and serve."[16] Paul was essentially referring to repentance by the Thessalonians when he said, "Ye turned to God from idols to serve the living and true God" (1 Thessalonians 1:9).

Saving faith follows true repentance. In fact, faith in the fullest sense embraces repentance as an essential part. Early theologians commonly held faith to involve, first, the assent of the mind; second, an act of the will; and, third, a restful trust in the faithfulness of God and the promises of His Word. The first element is involved in receiving the Word, as has already been discussed. The second element includes repentance, a whole-hearted turning from all sin to be a servant of God. It is only after such repentance has occurred that the soul is ready to rest in the faithfulness of God to keep His promise. So many of the promises of God are conditioned on human participation that trust is not possible until the conditions are met. From the Old Testament there are such promises as "Let the wicked forsake his way, and the unrighteous man his thoughts: and let him return unto the Lord, and he will have mercy upon him; and to our God, for he will abundantly pardon" (Isaiah 55:7); and "He that covereth his sins shall not prosper: but whoso confesseth and forsaketh them shall have mercy" (Proverbs 28:13). From the New Testament we have, "Repent ye therefore, and be converted, that your sins may be blotted out, when the times of refreshing shall come from the presence of the Lord" (Acts 4:19), and "If we confess our sins, he is faithful and just to forgive us our sins, and to cleanse us from all unrighteousness" (1 John 1:9). Many more could be given, but this is sufficient to establish the point. There are conditions to be met, and the sinner cannot truly trust God for salvation until he has forsaken his sinful ways, uncovered his sins before God in confession and turned to be an obedient follower of his Lord and Savior.

Yet saving faith is not faith in our own repentance or in our believing, but in the faithfulness of God to forgive sins and to bestow eternal life, on the basis of the sacrifice of Christ for us. In the act of faith, prevenient grace with its enablement passes over into saving grace with its regenerating power. Old things pass away; Christ enters into the life of the believer; and all things become new. Here is how Wesley described it:

> Faith is a divine *evidence* and *conviction*, not only that "God was in Christ, reconciling the world unto himself," but also that Christ loved *me*, and gave himself for *me*. It is by this faith . . . that we *receive Christ*; that we receive him in all his offices, as our Prophet, Priest, and King. It is by this that he is "made of God unto us wisdom, and righteousness, and sanctification, and redemption" . . .
>
> This faith necessarily implies an *assurance* . . . that Christ loved me, and gave himself for me. For "he that believeth" with the true living faith, "hath the witness in himself."[17]

A number of important things happen at once when a sinner trusts in Christ as His Savior: election, justification, regeneration, initial sanctification, and incorporation into the body of Christ, to name a few. There can then be no temporal order involved, only a logical one. We have not time for a full discussion of each element, but it is important to point out the contrasts with Calvinism.

Election unto salvation occurs as the sinner believes in Jesus Christ as his Savior. Calvin taught unconditional election from eternity, as has already been shown (Chapter 4). Individual election is from eternity in the sense that God foresees who shall believe and comply with the terms of salvation; it is actualized at the moment of saving faith in Jesus Christ. As Wiley summarized, "The elect are chosen, not by absolute decree, but by acceptance of the conditions of the call. And as the character of the elect consists of holiness and blamelessness before Him in love, so election is by those means which make men righteous and holy."[18]

Justification is that merciful and judicial act of God, whereby He forgives the sins of those who exercise faith in the propitiatory sacrifice of Christ in His death and declares them to be righteous in His sight.[19] Two facts stand out in contrast with the Calvinistic position. First, the imputation which is involved in justification is the imputation of faith for righteousness, and is applicable only so long as faith is genuine—so long as it is accompanied by sincere obedience. Thirteen times in the New Testament the Greek word *logizomai*, translated "to reckon, count, or impute," is used in connection with righteousness, and in nine of them it is used specifically in relation to faith. "Abraham believed God, and it was counted to him for righteousness" (Romans 4:3, 9, 22; Galatians 3:6; James 2:23). "To him that worketh not, but believeth on him that justifieth the ungodly, his faith is counted for righteousness" (Romans 4:5).

The righteousness received by faith is strictly the righteousness of God, and not our own. Wesleyans are so emphatic at this pint, just as Calvinists are. John Wesley commented on his Notes on the latter part of 2 Corinthians 5:21 ("For he hath made him to be sin for us, who knew no sin; that we might be made the righteousness of God in him"), saying, "Might *through him* be invested with that righteousness, first imputed to us, then implanted in us, which is in every sense *the righteousness of God.*"

The righteousness of God in Christ is both imputed and imparted to the believer, as Wesley declared. The expression "be made the righteousness of God" is in the present tense, indicating an ongoing progress. While imparted, or implanted righteousness brings the believer progressively nearer to "the measure of the stature of the fulness of Christ" (Ephesians 4:13), and while growing believers frequently perform below the level of Christ's absolute righteousness, so long as their faith is genuine and continuing, He is their surety before the throne of God, and "he is able also to save them to the uttermost that come unto God by him, seeing he ever liveth to make intercession for them" (Hebrews 7:22, 25).

When faith fails and willful disobedience occurs, there is no longer any imputation of Christ's merits to the sinner's credit. "If we sin willfully after we have received the knowledge of the truth, there remaineth no more sacrifice for sins, but a certain fearful looking for of judgment and fiery indignation, which shall devour the adversaries" (Hebrews 10:26-27). This is in striking contrast to the Calvinistic view of a once-for-all imputation of Christ's merits to the believer's account while he continually lives in sin.

Let it immediately be said that this does not make faith a work of merit. For if faith were a righteous act—an act of merit—it would not be *counted for righteousness*. Actual human righteousness and imputed righteousness are generally two different things; and, since faith is imputed for righteousness, it is not actual righteousness.

Justifying faith has God as its object, because of what He has said, and what he has provided through the death and resurrection of Jesus Christ. "To [us faith] shall be imputed, if we believe on him that raised up Jesus our Lord from the dead; who was delivered for our offenses, and was raised again for our justification" (Romans 4:23-24). Christ in His death provides the basis for our justification. In His life, He gives to us the Spirit of grace whereby we are enabled to exercise faith and walk in obedience.

When we believe, and because we believe, in God's saving provision through Christ, God as a merciful Sovereign forgives us all past sins; as Supreme Judge He counts us righteous as if we had never once sinned. Wesley called this a "wholesome doctrine, and very full of comfort." Indeed it is!

Second, justification is always accompanied by the beginning of sanctification. Justification includes forgiveness of all past sins and the imputation of righteousness; sanctification involves the impartation of righteousness. Wesley put it this way:

> What is justification?... It is evident, from what has been already observed, that it is not the being made actually just and righteous. This is *sanctification*; which is,

> indeed in some degree, the immediate fruit of justification, but nevertheless, is a distinct gift of God, and of a totally different nature. The one implies what God does for us through his Son; the other, what he works in us by his Spirit. So that, although some rare instances may be found, wherein the term *justified* or *justification* is used in so wide a sense as to include *sanctification* also; yet, in general use, they are sufficiently distinguished from each other, both by St. Paul and the other inspired writers.[20]

Justification is a change in our relationship to God; sanctification is a change in our state. But the latter always accompanies the former and is an evidence that the former has truly occurred. A faith that truly justifies is a faith that worketh by love, as Wesley insisted (Gal. 5:6). Any type of faith that does not bring such inward sanctification that a truly righteous life begins is not justifying faith. As James explained, "Was not Abraham our Father justified by works, when he had offered Isaac his son on the altar? Seest thou how faith wrought with his works, and by works was faith made perfect? And the scripture was fulfilled which saith, Abraham believed God, and it was imputed unto him for righteousness: and he was called the friend of God. Ye see then how that by works a man is justified, and not by faith only . . . . For as the body without the spirit is dead, so faith without works is dead also" (James 2:21-26). This does not mean that human works are the basis of justification, but that works of righteousness must follow justification if it is genuine. Otherwise, the faith which was exercised was dead presumption and not saving faith. There is no truly saving faith that does not express itself in righteous living.

Regeneration was defined by Wesley in the following words:

> It is that great change which God works in the soul when he brings it into life; when he raises it from the death of sin to the life of righteousness. It is the change wrought in the whole soul by the almighty Spirit of God when it is "created anew in Christ Jesus"; When it is "renewed after the image of God, in righteousness and true holiness."[21]

It is expressed in various terms in the Bible: "begotten of God" (1 John 5:1); "begotten again" (1 Peter 1:3); "quickened together with Christ" (Ephesians 2:5); "a new creature" (2 Corinthians 5:17); "being born again" (John 3:3); "born of the Spirit" (John 3:6); "newness of life" (Romans 6:4); and "being partakers of the divine nature" (2 Peter 1:4). This mighty transformation involves all three persons of the Holy Trinity. It is by the power of God that the new life is imparted to the soul that is dead in sins, and it is His nature which we receive in the new birth. The very life of Jesus becomes the life of the new creatures. "Christ liveth in me," said St. Paul (Galatians 2:20). And it is the Holy Spirit, acting through and in harmony with the Word of God, Who imparts the life of Christ to the believer.

Two serious errors of Calvinism are corrected in the Wesleyan view of regeneration. First, the Calvinists have held that sinners are wholly passive in this work of God upon them. That is an aspect of *monergism*, which has been earlier described. The Bible clearly contradicts such a position, repeatedly declaring the conditions for being made new creatures in Christ. Sinners are commanded, "Repent ye, therefore, and be converted, that your sins may be blotted out, when the times of refreshing shall come from the presence of the Lord (Acts 3:19). They are told, "Seek ye the Lord while he may be found, call ye upon him while he is near: let the wicked forsake his way, and the unrighteous man his thoughts: and let him return unto the Lord, and he will have mercy upon him; and to our God, for he will abundantly pardon: (Isaiah 55:6-7). One more example gives the necessity of faith: "Believe on the Lord Jesus Christ, and thou shalt be saved" (Acts 16:31). If men are convinced that they have no personal responsibility for seeking after God, they are encouraged either to be careless about their own sinful condition or to despair because they have received no overpowering compulsion to repent and be saved.

The second error is that regeneration precedes faith and justification. Calvinism holds that the Holy Spirit conveys the irresistible grace of God to the sinner and so renews him that he is now able to exercise faith and be justified. While Wesleyans agree that a sinner, dead in trespasses and in sins, has no power in himself to rise up and come to God in faith, they hold that there is prevenient grace by which a sinner is enabled so far to exercise faith as to come to God in repentance, and receive justification. With this the Scriptures agree: "As many as received him, to them gave he power to become the sons of God, even to them that believe on his name" (John 1:12); "For ye are all the children of God by faith in Jesus Christ" (Galatians 3:26). One must believe in Jesus Christ, and receive Him into the heart, in order to be regenerated. All such commands convey a false impression if the sinner is really regenerated before he believes or repents.

In contrast with the Calvinist teaching, justification logically precedes regeneration and inward sanctification. In time they are simultaneous, but not in rational order. If regeneration and inward righteousness occurred first, then we would have the impossible case of believers who were cleansed and made righteous who still were under condemnation from God, not being yet justified. It is manifest, therefore, that justification precedes the inward change.

Initial sanctification is simultaneous with justification and regeneration. Sanctification involves cleansing, and the cleansing of which we now speak is from the pollution acquired through sinful activity. It is sometimes called the pollution from guilt and from acquired, as opposed to inherited, depravity. That there is such a cleansing is evidenced by the scriptures: "Wash you, make you clean; put away the evil of your doings from before mine eyes... though your sins be as scarlet, they shall be as white as snow; though they be red like crimson, they shall be as wool" (Isaiah 1:16, 18). "Be not deceived: neither fornicators, nor adulterers, nor effeminate... shall inherit the kingdom of God. And such were some of you: but ye are washed, but ye are sanctified, but ye are justified in the name of the Lord Jesus, and by the Spirit of our God" (1 Corinthians 6:9-11). The washing is involved in the sanctification, and both are accomplished at the same moment as the justification.

Entire sanctification is a distinctive doctrine of Wesleyanism. Whereas initial sanctification is cleansing from acquired depravity, entire sanctification is cleansing from inherited depravity. Wesley included both phases in the following statement, in answer to the question, "When does inward sanctification begin?"

> In the moment we are justified. The seed of every virtue is then sown in the soul. From that time the believer gradually dies to sin, and grows in grace. Yet sin remains in him; yea, the seed of all sin, till he is sanctified throughout in spirit, soul, and body.[22]

The scripture to which he referred is 1 Thessalonians 5:23-24, "And the very God of peace sanctify you wholly; and I pray God your whole spirit and soul and body be preserved blameless unto the coming of our Lord Jesus Christ. Faithful is he that calleth you, who also will do it." In expounding the theme, Wesley insisted that there is sanctifying grace available to the believer in this present life such that he is saved from all sin, inward and outward; he is made perfect in love; and this is accompanied within the heart of the believer in an instant.[23] With him a great host of saintly scholars have agreed.

There is not space in the present treatise to study this subject exhaustively. It is given some further consideration in Chapter 9. It must suffice here only to say that the Thessalonian believers were outstanding examples of Christian grace before the exhortation above was addressed to them; that the grace presented is to be accomplished instantaneously (the Greek aorist tense of the verb "sanctify" denotes a completed act); and that the exhortation is accompanied by a sure promise that God is faithful to provide entire sanctification for believers.

Calvin did not allow the possibility of such entire cleansing from all sin in this present life, and most Calvinists have agreed with him. While Arminius did grant the possibility, he did not make it a prominent doctrine in his teachings. Wesley strongly emphasized it and particularly the energizing presence of the Holy Spirit enabling believers to overcome sin.

The Mild Calvinist Position

There is no single position that can be called consistently the "Mild Calvinist" one. Rather, there are various shades of belief somewhere between strict Calvinism and strict Arminianism. The following analysis focuses on a number of beliefs which have been popularized within evangelical circles and which can properly be called "mild Calvinism."

Without question, the influence of Arminianism has been great in helping to bring about this retreat from high Calvinism. How it has happened was briefly explained in Chapter 1. It will be shown in the following study that this combination of Arminianism and Calvinism has resulted in some serious inconsistencies and other problems for accurate Scripture interpretation.

Retreat from High Calvinism

A number of the high Calvinistic theses have been abandoned in the newer position. For one, unconditional election has been rejected. Evangelicalism today, with few exceptions, proclaims the gospel message freely to all men and sincerely calls every hearer to repentance. If they will, they are enabled to believe in Jesus for their salvation.

As an example, here are the words of H. A. Ironside, once pastor of Moody Church in Chicago, and a widely-known speaker and writer,

> All men may have faith if they will; but alas, many refuse to hear the Word of God, so they are left in their unbelief. The Holy Spirit presents the Word, but one may resist His gracious influence. On the other hand, one may listen to the Word and believe it.[24]

The above quotation also rejects the Calvinistic tenet of irresistible grace, stating in reference to the Holy Spirit, "one may resist His gracious influence."

A limited atonement is also generally not supported among modern evangelicals. Another widely-respected advocate of a modified Calvinism was

Lewis Sperry Chafer. He wrote of Christ,

> He died as a substitute for someone else, and that some one else is each and every individual in all the lost world of mankind… "And he is the propitiation for our sins: and not for ours only, but also for the sins of the whole world" (1 John 2:2).
>
> In the clearest terms, this death is here said to be a substitution… It is something accomplished for every person and in such perfection as to be fully satisfying to the infinite God. In like manner these passages are characterized by such universal words as "all," "every man" and "the whole world." From this it must be believed that the death of Christ has already provided a great potential and provisional value for every guilty sinner, which is now awaiting his personal recognition.[25]

Not nearly so much emphasis is placed on total depravity of mankind today as was in the Calvinistic scheme. Chafer in his book on *Salvation*, from which the above quotation is taken, has a chapter on "God's Estimate of the Lost." Descriptive terms such as "lost," perishing," "condemned," "under the wrath of God," "blind," and "dead in trespasses and sins," are used, but "depravity" is not mentioned. This does not mean that Chafer did not believe in human depravity, for he surely did. It means, rather, that this concept does not receive the emphasis which once it did. It is not widely held today that depravity is God's justification for reprobating certain persons unconditionally and eternally to hell. Instead, while the whole world is considered lost and helpless without God, God is viewed as genuinely offering salvation to every person who will hear His voice and believe on Jesus Christ.

Inconsistencies

While refusing some of the tenets of Calvinism, many of the neo-Calvinists, nevertheless, hold to a number of propositions that are logically derived from those tenets. By doing this, they involve themselves in serious inconsistencies. A few of these will now be presented.

First, there is the inconsistent proposition that, although a sinner before his conversion is free to repent and believe in Jesus Christ for his personal salvation—and he is truly responsible to do so—yet, after his conversion, he is no longer free to act in unbelief and be finally lost. The first clause of the proposition agrees with Arminianism, that sinners are acted upon by the Holy Spirit and are enabled to repent and exercise saving faith in Jesus Christ. The latter part is a return to the concepts of unconditional election, irresistible grace, and their derivatives. The concept is expressed in different ways. Some people say that if a believer backslides, goes into deep and awful sins, and dies in such condition, it is evidence that he never truly believed in the beginning. Others declare that God will never permit a backslider to die in such case. He may live in a fallen state, but he can never die like that. Such a position means that unconverted sinners have free moral agency, but believers have lost it. Sinners can come to grace and be saved, but believers cannot depart from it and be lost. It is a strange confusion of doctrine which describes sinners as having a freedom which is taken away from believers.

There is a second inconsistency, that after once believing n Jesus Christ for salvation, a person is relieved from responsibility for sin. Perhaps no teacher would admit to such a position, for it sounds so dangerous and unscriptural. Yet it is implicit in statements which are made. The inconsistency lies in the idea that sinners are responsible for their sins, but believers, though they continue to sin, are no longer responsible for the sins they commit.

Examine this statement made by Dr. John R. Rice, former editor of "The Sword of the Lord," and author of many books and booklets:

The righteousness which I have as a Christian is really the righteousness of Christ which was charged to my account when I trusted in Him. My sins likewise were charged up to Christ, and He has already paid for them. When Christ died on the cross, He died for all the sins that I ever committed or ever will, though I had not yet been born. That one sacrifice had to be sufficient to pay for all sin, and there will never be another sacrifice for man's sins.

> So when I trusted Christ, I got forgiveness for all my sins and from that time on my sins are charged back to Christ and are not charged against me at all. That is what God means when He says, "Blessed are they whose iniquities are forgiven, and whose SINS ARE COVERED. Blessed is the man to whom the Lord WILL NOT IMPUTE SIN." That is the reason a Christian will not come into condemnation and will not even come into judgment as far as his soul's salvation is concerned.
>
> The security of my soul depends, then, not at all on my goodness for I am not good; but it depends on the righteousness of Christ and His faithful promises.[26] (Emphasis his.)

Rice also said, speaking of those who are saved, "all have sinned and do sin, day by day."[27] Doubtless his personal life was better than his doctrine, for he did not want to encourage sinning in the Christian's life. So he continued,

> Perhaps someone will say, then, that it does not matter how a Christian lives if there is no danger of losing his soul. How foolish and shortsighted such a statement! Would you say to my daughter that it does not matter how she lives since her position as my daughter is secure? True, she is my daughter; she always will

be. And I dare say that even my poor, human father love would not fail her, no matter what she did. But she could easily lose the sweet communion with her father, crush all his pride in her, and lose all the happiness which she now has.

So it is with God's children. Sin breaks the communion with the Father, takes away the joy of salvation and loses much of the reward a Christian might have.[28]

In that analogy the writer reveals that he is not willing to accept the implications of his own theology. For if he applies it in the case he uses for an illustration, he must say that the sins of his daughter are not "charged against her at all." If somebody else has fully satisfied every claim against her for her sins in advance, how could her misconduct have any effect whatever upon his relation to her? It is obvious in the analogy that he *would* in no wise effect his fellowship with her. If her misconduct were a condition by accident or deformity, it would intensify a father's concern and communion. If it breaks that communion, it is perfectly obvious that he holds her accountable for what she does. But this is just what he denies about the sinner who has been justified. His sins have already been "charged back to Christ and are not charged against me at all."

The same inconsistency appears in the writings of J. Dwight Pentecost, renowned professor at Dallas Theological Seminary. Speaking of the believer's justification, he said,

The one who is placed in Christ Jesus is made righteous in the sight of God. God looks upon the one who is in Christ as clothed upon with the very righteousness of Jesus Christ so that there is no fault, no guilt, no basis for condemnation; we have been made righteous in Christ…

And when God looks at us in our position in Jesus Christ, He does not see us in our weakness, ignorance, and immaturity; He does not see us as stumbling, faltering babes in Christ—He sees us with all of the perfection that belongs to Jesus Christ. Thus God can view us as mature and adult sons in His own family.[29]

Notice the emphasis of that paragraph: whatever a believer does, of stumbling, failing—and that certainly includes sinning—God does not see it. Instead, God sees the believer as perfect and mature in Christ. The only possible conclusion from that is that it does not matter at all in God's sight what the believer now does; God does not see him as he really is in himself, but as a mature, adult child of God.

Pentecost does not want to accept such a conclusion, so he writes of the practical life of a believer as follows:

The child of God recognizes that no day is lived in practical righteousness and holiness. We stumble and fall, in thought, word, and deed. There is sin of omission, and sin of commission, and we stand convicted before a holy and righteous

> God… The Spirit of God can convict the child of God of his unholiness and can bring him to the place of confession so that sin might be forgiven and the believer might be restored.[30]

We may properly ask, what does the Spirit convict a person for, if God does not see what he does? Does the Spirit see what the Father does not see, and is He working in conflict with the Father? If all the guilt of sin has already been placed upon Christ, and it has already been satisfactorily dealt with, why is the Spirit bringing up the matter now? Has He forgotten that God has already been fully satisfied about sins which the believer is now committing? Why should the believer confess and ask forgiveness for sins that have already been fully forgiven in advance? Has the Spirit forgotten that those sins have already been forgiven? And if sins have been once forgiven already, should a sinner ask that they be forgiven a second time? If they were truly forgiven, either when Christ died on the cross or when the sinner first believed on Him, do they need to be forgiven again when the sinner actually commits them? Did not God really forgive the first time? Such questions accent the serious contradiction of this mild Calvinistic position.

A third inconsistency is in the claim that the mild Calvinist position does not produce a light and casual view of sin in practice. Arminians frequently point out that when professed Christians are convinced that they will never come into condemnation for any sins committed, they are encouraged to practice sin. Mild Calvinists deny this, but they are inconsistent in so doing.

That claim is violated in human practice. Dr. Myron Boyd, radio preacher, author, and leader of the Free Methodist Church, was speaking one day with a believer. In the course of the conversation the believer said to Dr. Boyd, "Christ forgave all my past sins, present sins, and all the sins I am going to commit during my life… I don't expect to quit sinning just because I'm a Christian."[31] The sincere Calvinist would probably say that person was not a true believer, for if he were, he wouldn't have such a casual attitude toward sin. But whether or not he believed on Jesus Christ, he did believe the doctrine of satisfaction for sins—past, present and future—were already "charged to the account of Christ," and that God did not hold him responsible for those sins any more. Now if a person actually believes that and acts accordingly—as this young man surely did—is that evidence that he was not a true believer? In other words, if a person truly believes and practices mild Calvinist doctrine about the satisfaction for sins by Jesus Christ, can he not also be a true believer in Jesus at the same time?

If he cannot, then the doctrine is obviously under condemnation. If it is allowed that the young man was a true believer, then it is proven that the doctrine which he believed encouraged him to treat sin lightly.

Moreover, the mild Calvinistic teaching is self-contradictory at this point. Observe the claims of Chafer:

> Does not the doctrine of security license people to sin? Biblically, No; Experimentally, No. There is no greater incentive in holiness of life than to know one's own eternal position in Christ Jesus. It is, according to the Bible, God's superlative appeal for true, Christian living. To the question, "Shall we continue in sin that grace may abound?" the unregenerate would answer "yes;" for that would be the voice of the fallen nature; but the regenerate answer, "God forbid."[32]

Chafer says, "The new nature does not commit sin: the old nature can do nothing else."[33]

Calvinists consistently teach that regenerated persons retain the "fallen nature" until death. If, then, the fallen nature says "yes" to the question, "Shall we continue in sin?" that answer will come from within the heart of the believer. And it is not sufficient motivation to overcome the fallen nature simply to be told that "in Christ" the believer has nothing to fear from sin. The fallen nature will be greatly encouraged by such reasoning, to continue the practice of sin which it so dearly loves and from which it can never cease.

Arminians teach, with the Scriptures, that there is a real danger of falling away from grace through willful sin and unbelief. They provide two motivations to holy living: positively, the desire to please God and gain His approval; and negatively, a sincere warning against falling back into sin and being lost. Chafer's thesis is that to take away the negative motivation and leave only the positive is to provide the strongest possible motivation toward holy living: positive motivation alone is stronger than the two combined. Anybody who has raised children according to the biblical pattern knows that to remove all fear of punishment—negative motivation—is not to produce the strongest possible motivation toward righteous living. Yet Chafer says, "To know our perfect standing in Christ does not lead to laxity in daily life: it is the strongest possible incentive to holy living that human heart can know."[34] That is contrary to established psychological principles of motivation.

Errors in Discipline

Another serious problem of the mild Calvinists, in addition to the inconsistencies already analyzed, is their identification of sin with the human nature and, particularly, with the body. Pentecost wrote, "We recognize that as long as we are in the flesh, we are living in an unredeemed body. We are living with an unredeemed sin-nature within us..."[35] He thus identified the sin-nature with an "unredeemed body," as if the body were as essentially evil as sin within the body.

Other writers have made sin virtually identical with the entire self, so that to be delivered from sin would necessitate the destruction of the self. For example, F. B. Meyer said, "The philosophy of the Bible is to do away with self, and to make Christ all in all."[36]

The Bible does not condemn the human nature, or the body, or the self as inherently evil. It is sin within the personality, and attaching itself to each aspect of that personality, which is unredeemed. Our bodies are to be the temples of the Holy Ghost, and we are to glorify God as consistently in the body as in the spirit (1 Corinthians 6:19-20). The entire personality—body, soul and spirit—is to be sanctified wholly (1 Thessalonians 5:23). St. Paul exhorted, "Let us cleanse ourselves from all filthiness of the flesh and spirit, perfecting holiness in the fear of God" (2 Corinthians 7:1).

"God sending his own Son in the likeness of sinful flesh, and for sin, condemned sin in the flesh" (Romans 8:3). It is not the flesh that was condemned, but sin in the flesh. The New Testament consistently gives respect to the human body as the creation of God which can be cleansed and used to His glory.

The common error of treating the body as essentially vile is similar to the Gnostic heresy of Bible times, with which New Testament writers had to deal. That error considered all material things as unalterably evil, while things of the spirit were considered good, potentially or actually. Chafer's statement, quoted earlier, that "the new nature does not commit sin: the old nature can do nothing else" is an echo of that ancient Gnosticism. The New Testament concept of wholeness in Christ is a radical departure from such a view of spiritual schizophrenia.

There is no suggestion in the Word that the "self" is to be destroyed in order for Christ to take control. Instead, sin is to be destroyed through the cross, so the self can be yielded unto God for sacred service (Romans 6:6, 13).

The mild Calvinistic teaching about the inevitability of sin is essentially a declaration that Jesus came to change the nature of sin rather than the nature of the sinner. No writer would say that explicitly, but it follows as a logical consequence of their position that believers may be justified while continuing to commit sin, without fear of coming into judgment for those sins. If the believer can still go on sinning without facing death as a result, then Jesus has removed danger from the believer's sins and has not taken sin away from the believer. In short, He has changed sin and not the sinner. The sinner is a sinner still, even after becoming a believer; but sin is no longer deadly to the believing "sinner." Such a position, being entirely unbiblical, is a dangerous position to adopt or to follow.

While the first four of the classic Calvinist tenets are either denied or minimized by the mild Calvinists, the last one—unconditional eternal security of the believer—is maintained assiduously. Wesleyans generally believe that insistence on the last tenet without the logical foundation of the other four is not only illogical, but is unscriptural as well. In the next chapter this subject will be explored.

Endnotes

1. In the English language the five points can be easily remembered by noticing that the initial letters combine to form the word "TULIP."
2. *Institutes*, II:iii:6.
3. Williamson, *Op. cit.*, p. 88.
4. *Westminster*, X:2.
5. Williamson, *Op. cit.*, p. 97.
6. Pentecost, *Op. cit.*, pp. 70-71.
7. *Institutes*, III:xiv:11, 12.
8. Wesley, *Works*, VIII, p. 430.
9. Adam Clarke, *Clarke's Commentary* (New York: Abingdon Press, n.d.), Vol. VI, p. 439.
10. William Burt Pope, *A Compendium of Christian Theology* (New York: Phillips and Hunt, 1880), Vol. II, pp. 358-59.
11. Mildred Bangs Wynkoop, *Foundations of Wesleyan-Arminian Theology* (Kansas City, MO: Beacon Hill Press, 1967), p. 105.
12. Joseph Henry Thayer, *A Greek-English Lexicon of the New Testament* (Grand Rapids, MI: Baker Book House, 1977 reprint), p. 484.
13. *Ibid.*, p. 130.
14. D. D. Whedon, *Commentary on the New Testament* (Salem, OH: Schmul Publishers, 1977 reprint), Vol. IV, p. 369.
15. Wesley, *Works*, VIII, p. 47.
16. J. Kenneth Grider, *Repentance unto Life* (Kansas City, MO: Beacon Hill Press, 1965), p. 64.
17. Wesley, *Works*, VI, p. 47.
18. Wiley, *Op. cit.*, Vol. II, pp. 338-39.
19. See Arminius, *Op. cit.*, Vol. I, pp. 598-99, and Wesley, *Op. cit.*, Vol. V, p. 57, for their respective definitions.
20. Wesley, *Works*, V, p. 56.
21. *Ibid.*, VI, p. 71.
22. *Ibid.*, VIII, p. 285.
23. *Ibid.*, pp. 294-96.

24. H. A. Ironside, *Full Assurance* (Chicago: The Moody Press, 1937), pp. 98-99.

25. Chafer, *Op. cit.*, pp. 32-33.

26. John R. Rice, *Can A Saved Person Ever Be Lost?* (Murfreesboro, TN: Sword of the Lord Publishers, 1943), p. 23.

27. *Ibid.*, p. 22.

28. *Ibid.*, p. 23.

29. Pentecost, *Op. cit.*, pp. 105-107.

30. *Ibid.*, p. 119.

31. Myron F. Boyd, *Honoring the Spirit* (Winona Lake, IN: Light and Life Hour, n.d.), p. 24.

32. Chafer, *Op. cit.*, pp. 112-113.

33. *Ibid.*, p. 102.

34. *Ibid.*, p. 74.

35. Pentecost, *Op. cit.*, pp. 119-20.

36. F. B. Meyer, *The Christ Life for the Self Life* (Chicago: Moody Press, n.d.), p. 45.

7

The Believer's Security

No other issue arising from Calvinism is of wider interest today than that of "eternal security" or the perseverance of the saints. The true Calvinists still maintain this tenet as a logical part of their theology. The various modifications of Calvinism, while minimizing or even abandoning other tenets, have generally held firmly to this one, even when its logical foundations have been removed. Many believers who are more Arminian than Calvinistic in their faith are nevertheless strongly attached to "the unconditional security of the believer."

As usual, we will view this doctrine from three perspectives.

The Calvinistic Position

John Calvin did not give so much emphasis to the eternal security of the believer as he did to the doctrines of divine sovereignty and unconditional election. As we shall see, he was somewhat troubled by the doctrine of perseverance. Even so, he did believe and teach it. In the *Institutes* he wrote,

> It cannot be doubted, that since Christ prays for all the elect, he asks the same thing for them as he asked for Peter—*viz.* that their faith fail not (Luke 22:32). Hence we infer, that there is no danger of their falling away, since the Son of God who asks that their piety may prove constant, never meets with a refusal. What then did our Savior intend to teach us by this prayer, but just to confide, that whenever we are his our eternal salvation is secure?[1]

Logical Necessity

Within Calvin's theological system there was nothing arbitrary about the doctrine of perseverance; it followed as a necessary conclusion from the premises of divine sovereignty, predestination and election. If God has willed to choose certain people—the elect—to be eternally saved, and if His absolute sovereignty guarantees the accomplishment of His will, then it follows necessarily that the elect can never be lost.

Perseverance, therefore, like the other tenets of Calvinism, arose out of philosophical considerations rather than from the Scriptures. As was shown in Chapter 1, this priority of philosophical presuppositions over the Scriptures has characterized Calvinism from its beginning. Augustine derived his doctrine of predestination in that way and sought to support it with Scripture. Calvin used the same approach. In the preface to his 1559 edition of the *Institutes*, he wrote, "I have given such a comprehensive summary and orderly arrangement of all the branches of religion, that, with proper attention, no person will find any difficulty in determining what ought to be the principle objects of his research in the Scriptures, and to what end he ought to refer anything it contains."[2] This plainly means that laymen in reading the Scriptures are to interpret them according to Calvin's doctrine.

James Arminius encountered the same priority of doctrine at Leyden University. Gomarus, the professor of New Testament studies, insisted that the Scriptures should always be interpreted according to the creed, while Arminius held to God's Word as the final authority.

The doctrine of security, then, was not derived from the Bible but from philosophical and logical considerations.

The Problem of Security

Calvin was too pious himself and too respectful toward God's Word to permit a casual disregard for sin in the believer's life. He recognized that there can be no deliverance from eternal death apart from faith (III:ii:1), and not true faith without obedience. ("Not only does faith, full and perfect faith, but all correct knowledge of God, originate in obedience," I:vi:2.) It follows that a disobedient person is not delivered from eternal death.

Yet Calvin believes that salvation was decreed of God for the elect entirely apart from any foreknowledge of their obedience. He thus has a conflict within his system of doctrine, which he labored to reconcile. His labor was not successful, as we may observe in the following quotation:

> None are enlightened unto faith, and truly feel the efficacy of the Gospel, with the exception of those who are foreordained to salvation, yet experience shows that the reprobate are sometimes effected in a way so similar to the elect, that even in their own judgment there is no difference between them… It is correctly said, that the reprobate believe God to be propitious to them, inasmuch as they accept the gift of reconciliation, though confusedly and without true discernment; not that they are partakers of the same faith or regeneration with the children of God; but because… they seem to have a principle of faith in common with them. Nor do I even deny that God illumines their minds to this extent, that they recognize his

> grace; but that conviction he distinguishes from the peculiar testimony which he gives to his elect in this respect, that the reprobate never obtain to the full result or the fruition. When he shows himself propitious to them, it is not as if he had truly rescued them from death, and taken them under his protection. He only gives them a manifestation of his present mercy. In the elect alone, he implants the living root of faith, so that they persevere even to the end.[3]

Let us review this lengthy passage to discover its amazing conclusion. 1) The operations of God upon the elect and the reprobate are frequently so similar that the two groups are alike in their own judgment. 2) The reprobate may believe they are reconciled unto God and delivered from death. They have a principle of faith; they recognize God's grace. In short, they may believe themselves to be among the elect, and this because of an illumination from God. 3) Yet in the reprobate, there is only a manifestation of *present mercy*. This differs from the mercy shown to the elect in one particular: the latter are enabled to persevere unto the end, whereas the reprobate are not because God's mercy is withdrawn from them. "The Lord, the better to convict them, and leave them without excuse, instills into their mind such a sense of his goodness as can be felt without the Spirit of adoption."[4]

Here is the conclusion that follows from Calvin's reasoning: one cannot be certain of his election until he has persevered unto the end! We can hardly call that a doctrine of security at all. It seems, rather, a doctrine of insecurity. God gives certain people enough mercy, faith and grace that they believe they are among the elect, then later withdraws the same to "leave them without excuse," condemned with the reprobate.

Calvin was not alone in his belief. Many Calvinist theologians have taken essentially the same position. Charles Hodge, for example, said, "The only evidence of election is effectual calling, that is, the production of holiness. And the only evidence of the genuineness of the call and the certainty of our perseverance is a patient continuance in well doing."[5] Concerning this statement, Shank has commented, "In other words, the only real evidence of election is perseverance, and our only assurance of the certainty of persevering is—to persevere!"[6]

The Mild Calvinistic Position

Under this term we now include all those who have departed from strict Calvinism but who still hold to unconditional security for the believer. Among them are many evangelicals who seldom, if ever, stress any of the other tenets of

Calvinism: total depravity, unconditional election, limited atonement or irresistible grace. They are considerably closer to Arminianism than to Calvinism.

There are three serious problems with this modified Calvinism, which will now be considered.

The Problem of Logical Inconsistency

As was stated in Chapter 1, large groups of evangelicals have abandoned some, if not all, of the first four tenets of Calvinism, while retaining the last one, perseverance of the saints. This involves them in serious inconsistency.

Within the present chapter it has been shown that the doctrine of unconditional eternal security, or the inevitable perseverance of the saints, was a necessary conclusion of a logical system derived not from the Scriptures but from certain philosophical presuppositions. It should be perfectly evident that if those presuppositions are neglected or denied, as they now are among a great many evangelicals, then the conclusion is no longer logically necessary. To insist on unconditional eternal security of the believer, while neglecting or denying unconditional election and irresistible grace, is like trying to hold up the roof of a house when the foundation and some or all of the walls have been removed.

The proponents of eternal security are doing more than advancing a doctrine lacking logical support, however. They are involving themselves in logical inconsistency as well. Let us now observe how this is true.

When evangelicals preach a gospel invitation to all men and declare that people are genuinely free to receive or reject it, they are denying the Calvinistic concepts of unconditional election, limited atonement and irresistible grace. And when these same evangelicals say that once a person has received Christ through a free, voluntary act of faith he is no longer free to renounce Christ through a voluntary act of unbelief and disobedience, they are taking a position unsupported by Calvinism, the Bible or sound reason. The high Calvinists were at least consistent when they asserted that the reprobate are not free to receive Christ and the elect are not free to reject Him. The modern "eternal security people" have abandoned that consistency when they declare that sinners are free to receive Christ (through the aid of the Spirit), but once having believed they are no longer free to reject Him (through resisting the Spirit). To imply that saving grace deprives individuals of one of the fundamental attributes of their humanity, their moral freedom, is entirely unreasonable and unsupported by Scripture.

Such teachers do not generally give forthright denials of freedom for the believer, even though their teaching implies such a denial. In fact, their interpretation of the atonement is such that the believer is still free to sin without any fear that his sin will separate him from Christ. The satisfaction theory of the atonement was explained in Chapter 5. According to this view, the believer is not separated from Christ by his sin. Although he is not excused for committing sin, he still has the volitional power to do so. He is thus free to sin, but not free to be separated from Christ.

People who hold this modified view, while they minimize the rigid tenets of Calvinism in their sincere proclamation of the gospel to all men, nevertheless return to those tenets, in effect, when they proclaim unconditional, eternal security for the believer. If the believer is not free to renounce Christ, then for him God's grace is irresistible. And if a person who once believe in Christ cannot effectively resist the will of God and terminate his faith in Christ, then over him God is exercising absolute sovereignty; he is predestined to everlasting life regardless of any merit or future conduct of his. He is among God's elect, and from this point on, at least, his election is unconditional.

Moreover, by adopting the satisfaction theory of the atonement, which assures believers of eternal life regardless of sinful practices, the modified Calvinists are returning to the doctrine of a limited atonement, for the satisfaction theory logically demands a limited atonement. If Christ fully satisfied the law's demands for any group of individuals—we may call them the elect, believers, or something else—and if they are assured of eternal salvation on the basis of that satisfaction, then either the satisfaction must apply to all men or the atonement must be limited to the applicable group of individuals. The modified Calvinist may reply that the satisfaction of Christ is applicable only to believers. But it must be evident to all thoughtful persons that the satisfaction of Christ is limited either by the scope of the atonement as God has decided it or by the exercise of human faith; it cannot be both. Now if it is limited by human faith, then the atonement applies to a believer, and it does not apply to an unbeliever. This is true even if the same person is at one time a believer and later an unbeliever. Otherwise faith is not the determining factor; the sovereign decree of God is, and we have returned to a limited atonement.

The same reasoning can be applied to the concept of election. If it is determined by individual faith, then unbelievers, though once saved, are no longer included. If it is determined by divine decree, then we have unconditional election.

To summarize the foregoing discussion: those who hold to a belief in unconditional eternal security for believers must, if they are consistent, hold also to the Calvinistic tenets of unconditional election, limited atonement, irresistible grace, and back of them all the absolute sovereignty of God. Yet there are many good and sincere persons who hold to eternal security while denying some, or all, of the other tenets of Calvinism. Evidently they have not yet recognized their inconsistency.

The Problem of Creed versus Scripture

We have already observed that the doctrine of unconditional eternal security was derived as a conclusion in a logical system whose presuppositions were philosophical rather than biblical. When conflicts appeared, as in the disagreement between Gomarus and Arminius, the Calvinists gave priority to creed rather than to Scriptures. In broad areas of modern evangelicalism, the Calvinistic presuppositions have been forsaken, yet the conclusion is held tenaciously. Since the logical support has been stripped away, the modern proponents endeavor to support from the Scriptures a doctrine which was not derived from them in the first place. In order to do so, they must repeat the old Calvinistic practice of giving priority to creed when it conflicts with Scriptures.

While it would be difficult to find a frank admission by any proponent of eternal security that the Scriptures are being twisted into an agreement with their doctrine, careful observers may easily detect that this is being done. The observations of Dr. William W. Adams, retired professor of New Testament Interpretation at the Southern Baptist Theological Seminary of Louisville, Kentucky, may serve to illustrate the fact. In 1960 Robert Shank, a Baptist minister trained in the doctrine of unconditional eternal security, published *Life in the Son*, in which he gave a most scholarly refutation of the doctrine. In the introduction to the volume Dr. Adams wrote a warning to the author:

> Some will loudly denounce your book merely because you dare to call in question some of their customary interpretations and to challenge their accustomed doctrinal position. They will label you a heretic or a novice...
>
> Some will consider that "unity" is more important than truth and that, right or wrong, conformity to tradition and popular opinion is the only wise course. Men so easily become enslaved by a vested interest in the *status quo,* and *many will refuse to venture the risk of honestly searching for truth at the possible expense of comfort.*
>
> ...But this much is assured: all genuine scholars and searchers after truth will be compelled to take your book into consideration[7] (Emphasis added).

Ten years later, Shank wrote a companion volume, *Elect in the Son*, in which he fully supported the view of conditional election. Again Dr. Adams wrote the introduction, and he made two significant assertions. First, he declared,

> ...nothing of consequence has been offered against *Life in the Son* in the ten years since its publication.
>
> ...It is my considered judgment that Robert Shank's two books *Life in the Son* and *Elect in the Son* will stand against any attempt to refute them from the Scriptures.[8]

Second is the fact that leaders of the Baptist convention excluded him from fellowship with their churches because of his doctrinal position. This, Dr. Adams called "the ill-conceived actions of men in positions of authority in the ecclesiastical structure of his denomination."[9]

Here is the admission by a Baptist theologian that one of their own men was forced out of the denomination after demonstrating that the unconditional security position is in error. The leaders who forced him out could not prove him wrong from the Scriptures, but removed him anyway because he departed from their doctrine.

As a further illustration of the priority of creed, we may observe how various writers treat Hebrews 6:4-6, "For it is impossible for those who were once enlightened, and have tasted of the heavenly gift, and were made partakers of the Holy Ghost, and have tasted the good word of God, and the powers of the world to come, if they shall fall away, to renew them again unto repentance; seeing they crucify to themselves the Son of God afresh, and put him to an open shame." Some writers insist that this passage refers to people who have never been saved at all; others admit that the strong descriptive terms must refer to truly regenerated people. Within the latter group, there is further disagreement. Some allow that, theoretically, the regenerated could apostatize and be lost, but that actually the biblical warning will prevent their doing so. Others insist that apostasy is not involved, but only minor backsliding, from which there can be recovery without renewal of the foundation of repentance.

Not more than one of the explanations can be true, and all might be false. Each writer is satisfied with his presentation, however, because it supports the eternal security doctrine. The criterion of adequacy is not to find what the passage really says, but to make it say something in harmony with the doctrine.

In support of this statement let us examine the explanation of one author who defends the last-stated alternative; that is, that Hebrews 6:4-6 refers to the backsliding—but not apostasy—of those who were truly regenerated. He says,

> A careful examination of the four descriptive phrases (vv. 4-5) makes it very difficult to believe that they are not describing people who have been born anew...
>
> This has been a difficult verse to me as to many others. As I could not conceive of the believer's security in Christ being challenged by the verse as it stood, I was much inclined to accept the customary view in spite of its deficiencies and without being fully satisfied with it...
>
> *It is impossible to lay foundations twice over*. It is an impossibility in the nature of the case; a foundation is something that cannot be continually laid again. And the people described here are those who already have the foundation...of the new birth. It is impossible to lay that foundation again, simply because it is already there...

After declaring that "falling away" is simply "side-slipping," which can easily happen to a believer, the writer continues,

> There is no need for him to go back to the foundation of initial repentance, but rather he is to count his backslidden works as doomed to be burned and go on to perfection, full growth, leaving what chastening may be involved in the hands of his heavenly Father..."[10]

The "customary view" to which the writer refers involves two propositions: 1) the people described were never born of God; and 2) their "falling away" is genuine apostasy, which ends in eternal loss. They did not fall away from a position of true faith, but from a merely nominal profession of faith. The writer under consideration did not accept the first proposition as true; he was convinced from the Word that the people described were truly born of God.

To deny the first proposition and still accept the second placed him in a difficult position, however. As he expressed it, he "could not conceive of the believer's security in Christ being challenged by the verse as it stood." He thus admits that the verse, *as it stands*, contradicts unconditional eternal security. But since this is inconceivable, the verse must not be permitted to remain as it stands. It must be forced into agreement with the doctrine! The writer was finally able to accomplish this by denying the second proposition. The "falling away" applies to believers without threatening their security in Christ.

Most commentators allow that real apostasy was the danger faced by the Hebrew Christians; so, to keep their interpretation in harmony with eternal-security doctrine, they insist that the persons in danger of apostasy were not born of God. A true believer would not be in danger of apostasy even if he yielded to the temptation and renounced the entire gospel system.

Other commentators admit that if a true believer should renounce the gospel he would apostatize; but actually, by giving the warning, God prevents such an occurrence. The ruling principle for all of these commentators is to make the passage fit their doctrine rather than to let it remain "as it stands" in conflict with that doctrine.

While considering the book of *Hebrews*, we may look at another problem passage, Hebrews 10:25-29. It speaks of the possibility that we sin willfully after that we have received the knowledge of the truth. It refers to the apostate who has "trodden under foot the Son of God, and hath counted the blood of the covenant, wherewith he was sanctified, an unholy thing, and hath done despite unto the Spirit of grace," and it promises to such people a sorer punishment than those received who died without mercy under Moses' law. They must look forward to a fearful judgment and fiery indignation, because there "remaineth no more sacrifice for sins."

Notice that the Hebrew writer includes himself among the "we" who were confronted with the temptation to willful sin and apostasy. The same group had been sanctified through the blood of the covenant. Certainly, such a group of people, who included the writer of the epistle, who had an experiential knowledge of the truth (for so the Greek word indicates), and who had been sanctified through the blood of Christ, were truly God's children. If the "we" passages of warning are followed through the epistle, the conclusion is compelling that children of God are involved.

A brilliant young scholar of the writer's acquaintance was converted and educated in an "eternal security" setting. He went to study for his doctorate in a widely-known, Christian university where the doctrine is upheld. In his candid searching of the Scriptures, however, he became more and more doubtful of the doctrine. Finally, when he came to this passage about those who have been sanctified through the blood of the covenant and the judgment which they face if they sin willfully, he renounced the security doctrine as a system of error.

Many teachers and writers do not come to this passage to learn from it, though; they approach it with the determination to force it into agreement with their doctrine. When the epistle says that certain people were sanctified, that cannot be permitted to mean that they were cleansed from sin and set apart unto God; it s rather interpreted as a merely external and formal sanctification which did not change their hearts. Such an interpretation overlooks the fact that elsewhere in the epistle "sanctified" refers to genuine Christians; but it is permitted as the best way to force the passage into harmony with a doctrine to which they are committed.

Seven times in this epistle, the terms "sanctify" and "sanctified" are used. One refers to Old Testament sacrifices (9:13), and six refer to the work which Christ performs in believers through His shed blood. When interpreters take the statement about those who were sanctified through the blood of the covenant and make it mean that they were not really sanctified, we wonder what kind of language the Bible could possibly use that *would* convince them of error in their doctrine. Such an attitude is not too surprising, though, when we remember that, historically, creed has been given priority over Scriptures in the Calvinistic tradition.

Before passing to another problem, we may observe three more examples of how clear scripture passages are changed in meaning to conform to the doctrine. First is John 10:27-29 and the use that is made of it:

> My sheep hear my voice, and I know them, and they follow me: and I give unto them eternal life; and they shall never perish, neither shall any man pluck them out of my hand. My father, which gave them me, is greater than all; and no man is able to pluck them out of my Father's hand.

Let us assert, thankfully, that this is a beautiful passage about the security of the believer. And let it be asserted also that Wesleyan-Arminians do not teach *insecurity* for the believer. They rejoice in every Bible passage which proclaims their assurance and security; and there are many of them. The crucial question is not whether the believer is secure or not, but whether that security is conditional or unconditional. We are now considering those who teach that security is unconditional and who use this Bible passage as a basis for the teaching.

This passage surely does teach security in the Father's hand. It shows that our Father is greater than any force or combination of forces that might endeavor to separate us from Him. In the immediate background is the story of a man born blind, who confessed his faith in Christ and who was consequently excommunicated from temple worship. In spite of that persecution, he believed in and worshiped Jesus Christ.

Again, the important question here concerns conditions. All evangelicals will surely agree that there is an initial condition of faith in Christ which brings a person into the place of security. We speak of the "security of the *believer*," not of the unbeliever. But does a person have to maintain that condition of faith in order to be preserved securely in the Father's hand? That is the decisive question. The eternal security proponents hold that there is no ongoing condition: once a person is a believer in the Father's hand, he is absolutely safe for all eternity, even if he returns to unbelief, rebellion, and unabated wickedness.

Look at the passage again. It says, "My sheep know my voice...and they follow me." The verbs "hear" and "follow" are in the present tense. The sheep continue to hear and continue to follow. Those who do not continue to hear and follow are not sheep. There is clearly an ongoing condition of hearing and following Jesus. In verse 26 Jesus aid to certain of the Jews, "Ye believe not because ye are not of my sheep." Unbelievers are not sheep, for sheep are believers.

We must conclude that this passage presents *conditional eternal security*. It says nothing whatever about those who were once believers but who later lapse into unbelief and sin. Those who use it to teach unconditional security are forcing it to say what it does not say, in order to support their position.

Having given the foregoing passage a meaning which is not justified, teachers frequently use it as a "proof text" in their interpretation of other passages. To illustrate: in his chapter on "The Eternal Security of the Believer," Chafer treats Revelation 22:19 as follows:

> "And if any man shall take away from the words of the book of this prophecy, God shall take away his part out of the book of life, and out of the holy city, and from the things that are written in this book." The warning is most general. That no child of God would be permitted to do this, or to come under this judgment, is assured in 1 Corinthians 10:13 and John 10:29.[11]

The passage declares that it is possible for people to lose their part in the book of life. Chafer denies that this can apply to a child of God but gives no better reason for his claim than a reference to John 10:29. (1 Corinthians 10:13 is no more of a support for unconditional security than John 10:29.) Repeatedly through his chapter he returns to John 10:29, ever using it in his effort to prove that the believer's security is unconditional. This, as we have seen, is wholly unjustified.

The second passage for examination is John 15:6, "If a man abide not in me, he is cast forth as a branch, and is withered; and men gather them, and cast them into the fire, and they are burned." It is truly amazing to behold the diversity of interpretations given to this verse! Chafer, for example, says,

> This difficult passage may best be understood in its probable relation to professors. The reference is to "a man" and not to a branch, as in verse 2. In such a case

> "abide not in me" could hardly mean more than a pretense, or false profession which "men" disallow as they would gather and burn dead branches.[12]

Charles C. Ryrie comments, "John 15:6, in the author's judgment, is a reference to the burning of useless works at the judgment seat of Christ (as in 1 Corinthians 3:15), but salvation is assured even though this happens."[201]

J. F. Strombeck observes, "In the One who said, 'Every branch in *me*,' there is lie in a universal sense. It is for *all* men. This life is on a purely human plane. It is not divine, nor is it eternal. In the figure, it is represented by the corruptible wood and leaves of the branches."[14]

And John R. Rice has said,

> A man may be out of touch with Christ after he has been saved and so cannot bear fruit; he may be withered and lose all the joy which he had, as Christians many times do... But notice in this verse that those which are gathered and cast into the fire are the branches cut from the grapevines, and not men at all...
>
> A withered branch, so worthless to men because it will not bear grapes and is therefore burned up, is used to show how useless is a Christian in God's service who does not abide in Christ... This Scripture does not teach that a saved person can be lost and does not say so.[15]

Behold the contradictions contained in these teachings! Chafer says the verse is about a man and not a branch; Rice says it is about branches and not men. Chafer says the man represents false professors; Ryrie and Rice say saved persons; and Strombeck says the whole world of sinful men. Chafer says the burning represents rejection by men of the world; Ryrie says the judgment of the believer's works by Christ. It is hardly necessary to refute such teachings, for they contradict each other. Yet the writers do not criticize each other for faulty interpretation of the scriptures. Instead, they join in criticizing those who reject their doctrinal position, which is upheld by doubtful interpretations.

Jesus was talking to His followers when He said, "Ye are the branches." Of them He also said, "Now ye are clean through the word which I have spoken unto you" (v. 3). This applied to none but children of God. The unfruitful branches are to be taken away. (Incidentally, some commentators say this means the unfruitful ones are taken to heaven. The Greek word is not the one used of Jesus, however, when He was *taken up* into heaven.) The same branches are cast forth and burned. They are no longer joined to Christ and can no more share His life. Once again, there is an evident condition to continuous security, and that is continued abiding in Christ.

The third passage for study is 2 Peter 2:18-22, which speaks of those who "were clean escaped from them who live in error"; and who "have escaped the pollutions of the world through the knowledge of the Lord and Savior Jesus Christ." It says of them that if "they are again entangled therein, and overcome, the latter end is worse with them than the beginning. For it had been better for them not to have known the way of righteousness, than after they have known it, to turn from the holy commandment delivered unto them. But it is happened unto them according to the true proverb, The dog is turned to his vomit again; and the sow that was washed to her wallowing in the mire."

The common way of evading the force of this passage is to press the figures of speech too far. John R. Rice, for example, says the dog is still a dog and the sow is still a sow, and God never calls His people either dogs or sows. He continues, "If God had made this sow into a sheep and changed her nature as He does the nature of one who is born again, the sheep would not have delighted in the mud like a sow…"[16]

This interpretation violates one of the most fundamental rules of Bible interpretation, that parable and similar figures can not be made to apply at every point. We must discover the lesson which the figure is designed to teach and not press it beyond that. In the figure of the sow, there is a physical washing; in the analogy, there is a spiritual washing, referred to in the words "they have escaped the pollutions of the world…"

Now when a sinner is washed from spiritual pollutions, he is in that very washing made a new creature in Christ Jesus. St. Paul speaks of the "washing of regeneration" (Titus 3:5), indicating that the washing and the regeneration (beginning of new life) are united together. It is therefore irrelevant to observe that the pig did not become a sheep when it was washed. Pigs *never* become sheep through washing, but sinners do become saints by the washing of regeneration. Parables and proverbs use familiar, earthly stories to illustrate spiritual truth. There would be nothing at all familiar about the notion that a washed pig should become a sheep; that *never* happens.

If there is to be anything else taken from the figure than the fact that a sinner once washed from pollution may return to it, it is that the pig still has a pig's nature—an inclination toward the unclean—even after it is washed. Likewise, a newly-regenerated person still has an inherited sinfulness of nature which attracts him toward sinful practice. It is this very fact which makes the warnings against backsliding so pertinent for immature believers.

The Problem of Antinomianism

The term means simply "against law." It was introduced by Martin Luther in opposition to the growing belief that faith in Christ releases a person from obligation to keep the moral law, especially as set forth in the Old Testament. Such an attitude has frequently been identified with groups which have had their roots in Calvinism and the Reformation. During the Wesleyan revival in England the problem became so acute that John Fletcher, the renowned Wesleyan theologian, wrote his forceful treatise, *Checks to Antinomianism*, to combat the evil.[17]

We have already observed in Chapter 6 that mild Calvinism tends to produce a casual, and even careless, regard for sin in a believer's life. That reasoning need not be repeated here. One illustration may suffice to establish the fact. John R. Rice wrote,

> How ashamed and heartsick will many a child of God be when Jesus comes, unexpectedly, and the Christian is found in sin. Some may be in theaters, some in taverns, and some engaged in business that will horribly embarrass them before Christ. Do not say no Christian ever goes where he should not. Many a Lot, vexing his righteous soul will be in the midst of some wicked Sodom when Jesus comes. Many a David after God's own heart in other matters may be with some Bathsheba when Jesus comes. Many a Peter will be warming by the devil's fire and denying his Lord. So we may expect the roofs of picture houses to need repair, broken by raptured but shameful Christians at the rapture, when Jesus comes for His own. For He will take His own. It will still be of grace, not of works, and we who deserve to be left behind, but have trusted in the blood shed for sinners, will be taken with our Savior, when He comes for those He has purchased. Christ will not seize an arm and a leg of His bride and leave the body here. It will be a rapture, not a rupture.[18]

If a person really believes such teaching—and it is wholly consistent with the doctrine of unconditional security—and if he further believes that daily sinning is inevitable—another tenet taught by Calvinists—the net result will certainly be a casual, permissive attitude toward sin.

Quickly let it be added that many evangelicals will object to such statements. They hate sin and they are endeavoring to live consistent, holy lives. The writer has personally known many such individuals, whose lives were beautiful examples of Christlikeness. This is because their life comes from the Spirit of Christ within them and not from their doctrine. In short, their lives are far ahead of their doctrine!

The fact remains that the security doctrine derived from Calvinism encourages permissiveness toward sin. In their zeal for holy living, adherents of the doctrine commonly insist that believers who lapse into gross sins have never been truly born of God. Hession, to take one example, has written,

> The proof that they were genuine would be that they would continue in His Word; if they did not so continue, then they were not the real thing at all...
>
> If a professed Christian does not depart from iniquity, but rather departs from the Lord, and that in the decisive way we have indicated, then we can only assume he is not one of "them that are his."[19]

It is a commonly-observed fact that professed believers do lapse into deep sin. This writer recalls the case of a worldly-minded young lady who came under the spiritual influence of godly young people and was soundly converted. She broke off her sinful relationships, enrolled in a Bible college, and became an enthusiastic witness for Christ. Upon completion of Bible college, she enrolled in a secular college to study psychology. There her faith was undermined and she returned to the old ways of unbelief and sin. Not long after her loss of faith, she suffered a suicide's death in violation of God's Word. Advocates of modified Calvinism must either say she was never a child of God, thus sacrificing her security as a believer, or she was still a child of God during her fall into unbelief, sin, and even self-murder. In the latter case, they are surrendering to antinomianism.

This young lady thought she was a believer. Her friends, both old and new, accepted her as a true believer. In fact, she *was* a believer. She confessed her sins, according to God's Word, left the old life, trusted Jesus Christ as her Savior, and witnessed enthusiastically to her life in Christ. If these actions do not bring a person to a place of security, what does? If after all of this, because of her death in sin, we are told she was never a true child of God at all, then what has become of the doctrine of security? If a person who acts like a believer and is confident of personal salvation is nevertheless insecure until death, then the doctrine of a believer's security is reduced to a treacherous mirage!

On the other hand, if it is held that such a person as the young lady was a child of God even until death, then an Antinomian position has been accepted. In summary, the modified Calvinists must either surrender unconditional security or surrender *to* antinomianism; no middle ground appears available.

The Wesleyan-Arminian Position

It must be repeated at the outset that Wesleyan-Arminians accept fully the biblical doctrine of security. They rejoice in all the sacred passages which assure that God protects and keeps His own, even to eternity. John Wesley wrote about Romans 8:38-39 thus: "The apostle was at that time fully persuaded of his own perseverance. And I doubt not, but many believers at this day have the same persuasion, termed in Scripture, 'The full assurance of hope,'" Then he continued, "But this does not prove that every believer shall persevere..."[20]

The Conditions of Eternal Security

Arminians are willing even to accept the concept of eternal security, so long as we qualify it as *conditional* rather than unconditional.

Let us observe what the conditions are. First is *faith.* All evangelicals recognize that faith is necessary for the beginning of salvation in the new birth. Arminians affirm that faith must continue as a condition of security.

It has already been stated that "believing" is generally in the present tense in the Greek New Testament, showing that faith must be continuously maintained.

One of the favorite passages of the unconditional securitists is John 5:24, "Verily, verily, I say unto you, He that heareth my word, and believeth on him that sent me, hath everlasting life, and shall not come into condemnation; but is passed from death unto life." The words "heareth" and "believeth" are both in the present tense, indicating an ongoing condition of hearing and believing. This verse says nothing whatever about those who cease hearing and believing, and it is an unwarranted interpretation to make it apply to them.

Another passage which reveals the faith condition is 1 Peter 1:3-5, "Blessed be the God and Father of our Lord Jesus Christ, which according to his abundant mercy hath begotten us again unto a lively hope by the resurrection of Jesus Christ from the dead, to an inheritance incorruptible, and undefiled, and that fadeth not away, reserved in heaven for you, who are kept by the power of God through faith unto salvation ready to be revealed in the last time." Arminians recognize that we are not kept by self-effort, but by the power of God. Yet this passage emphatically asserts that the keeping power of God operates "through faith." It has a condition which the kept ones must meet if they are to be kept.

It is readily acknowledged that a sinner must believe in Christ to be saved. Why should it be considered strange that a saved person must continue to believe in order to maintain the new relationship with God? It is both scriptural and reasonable that the condition for initial salvation must be maintained for present, ongoing salvation. In fact, we are kept by faith unto final salvation.[21]

Another condition of security is *continuing obedience*. We have already observed (Chapter 6) that saving faith cannot coexist with willful disobedience. Hence the condition of faith really includes the condition of obedience. But there are numerous scriptures which emphasize the necessity of obedience, some of which will be included here. "And hereby we do know that we know him, if we keep his commandments. He that saith, I know him, and keepeth not his commandments, is a liar, and the truth is not in him... He that saith he abideth in him ought himself also so to walk, even as he walked" (1 John 2:3, 4, 6). What a strong statement we have here! Those who say they know Him (perhaps because they once placed their trust in Him for salvation), and yet are not now keeping His commandments, are liars, and the truth is not in them!

Obedience to God involves holy living and total abstinence from specific actions and attitudes. One such specific is hatred for a brother: "Whosoever hateth his brother is a murderer: and ye know that no murderer hath eternal life abiding in him" (1 John 3:15). Whatever a person's past faith may have been, he cannot now possess eternal life if he is now hating his brother.

Another specific is forsaking the doctrine of Christ; that is, His divine-human personality as the Son of God incarnate. "Look to yourselves, that we love not those things which we have wrought, but that we receive a full reward. Whosoever transgresseth, and abideth not in the doctrine of Christ, hath not God. He that abideth in the doctrine of Christ, he hath both the Father and the Son" (2 John 8-9). The believers of John's day were under strong influence from the Gnostics to renounce the doctrine of Christ. He is addressing believers in this passage who will receive a full reward if they abide in the doctrine. If they transgress and forsake the doctrine, they no longer have God; they have gone over to the position of the antichrist. Howard Marshall comments,

> These verses express the possibility that John's readers may go astray and lose their salvation—and we note that this warning is addressed to people described as 'elect' (2 John 1). Hence we must allow the possibility that believers might lapse from the true faith through following false teachers, whether or not the group of teachers were themselves regarded as lapsed believers.[22]

One more specific is abstaining from lying. "But the fearful and unbelieving, and the abominable, and murderers, and whoremongers, and sorcerers, and idolaters, and all liars, shall have their part in the lake which burneth with fire and brimstone: which is the second death" (Revelation 21:8). "Blessed are they that do his commandments, that they may have right to the tree of life, and may enter in through the gates into the city. For without are dogs, and sorcerers, and whoremongers, and murderers, and idolaters, and whosoever loveth and maketh a lie" (Revelation 22:14-15). Here a number of sins, including lying, are specified as barring all who are guilty from the eternal city of God. It cannot be allowed, if we are true to the Word, that people who are doing these things can still be admitted to heaven because they once put their trust in Christ. These verses speak of "*all* liars," not just those who have never trusted Christ.[23]

In addition to the conditions of faith and obedience, there are frequent references to *continuing* in various graces of the Christian life. "Then Jesus said to those Jews which believed on him, If ye continue in my word, then are ye my disciples indeed" (John 8:31). "As the Father hath loved me, so have I loved you: continue ye in my love. If ye keep my commandments, ye shall abide in my love..." (John 15:9-10). "And...they returned again to Lystra, and to Iconium, and Antioch, confirming the souls of the disciples, and exhorting them to continue in the faith, and that we must through much tribulation enter into the kingdom of God" (Acts 14:21-22). "Behold therefore the goodness and severity of God: on them which fell, severity; but toward thee, goodness, if thou continue in his goodness: otherwise thou also shalt be cut off" (Romans 11:22). "And you, that were sometimes alienated and enemies in your mind by wicked works, yet now hath he reconciled in the body of his flesh through death, to present you holy and unblameable and unreproveable in his sight: if ye continue in the faith grounded and settled, and be not moved away from the hope of the gospel" (Colossians 1:21-23).

The grand security passage in Romans 8:35-39 has already been discussed in connection with predestination (Chapter 3). Even there, though, a condition is involved. Chapters 3 to 5 treat justification by faith; 6 to 8 concern inherited sin and full deliverance from it. In Chapter 8 glorification is considered, and we are assured that God has provided sufficient grace to preserve us to the end. The condition is given in verse 17, "The Spirit itself beareth witness with our spirit, that we are the children of God: and if children, then heirs; heirs of God, and joint-heirs with Christ; if so be that we suffer with him, that we may be also glorified together. For I reckon that the sufferings of this present time are not worthy to be compared with the glory which shall be revealed in us" (Romans 8:16-18). St.

Paul personally weighed the alternatives of present sufferings with future glory, on one hand, and present pleasures with future loss, on the other. He chose to endure suffering gladly, and he presents it as a condition for every believer to meet if he is to enjoy the glory to come: "if we suffer we may be glorified together."

God never makes this choice for any person. He presents the alternatives, but we are creatures of choice. We must make the right choice and maintain it. St. Paul knew people who made the right choice at first and later reversed it. Demas was one of them. He suffered affliction with Paul for an extended period, even in prison, and was one of Paul's approved fellow-laborers. That is a strong, though not a conclusive, indication that he was a true believer. Yet he returned to Thessalonica, "having loved this present world" (2 Timothy 4:10); and tradition tells us that he became a priest in an idol's temple there. Now "if any man love the world, the love of the Father is not in him" (1 John 2:15). Demas departed from the faith and loved this present world. He could not continue in the love of God. He reckoned that worldly pleasure was more to be desired than continued suffering with St. Paul, even though future glory was in prospect.

Hymenaeus and Alexander were two other individuals who departed from the faith. "War a good warfare; holding faith, and a good conscience, which some having put away concerning faith have made shipwreck: of whom is Hymenaeus and Alexander; whom I have delivered unto Satan, that they may learn not to blaspheme" (1 Timothy 1:18-20). The context includes strong warnings about danger from false teachers, who were "subverting...the hearers" (2 Timothy 2:14) and who "overthrow the faith of some" (2:18). Concerning the two men Marshall writes, "It has been suggested that 'they are said to have given up or to have made shipwreck of that faith which they never possessed except in appearance,' but this is very unlikely. The language suggests a violent rejection of the claims of conscience, and the metaphor of shipwreck implies the loss of a faith once held."[24] Marshall believes that the delivery unto Satan involved excommunication from the church, putting them back in Satan's kingdom as "captured deserters."

The believer must *continue to* refrain from sin and practice righteousness, if he is to remain a child of God. "What shall we say then? Shall we continue in sin, that grace may abound? God forbid. How shall we that are dead to sin live any longer therein? ... What then? shall we sin, because we are not under the law, but under grace? God forbid. Know ye not, that to whom ye yield yourselves servants to obey, his servants ye are to whom ye obey; whether of sin unto death, or of obedience unto righteousness?" (Romans 6:1-2, 15-16). In this passage Paul treats sinning not as an accident but as an act of self-surrender. He is certainly addressing himself to believers, and says that if they yield themselves to sin, it will bring death; they will again be the servants of sin.

There is perhaps no more dangerous element in modified Calvinism than the teaching about sin. We have already observed quotations which present their theory that when once born again a believer is no longer in danger of spiritual death, no matter how willfully, how often, or how flagrantly he sins. Such a view contradicts the repeated, forceful statements of scripture. John said, "Little children, let no man deceive you: he that doeth righteousness is righteous, even as he is righteous. He that committeth sin is of the devil; for the devil sinneth from the beginning. For this purpose the Son of God was manifested, that he might destroy the works of the devil" (1 John 3:7-8). Yet today many "little children" are being deceived by those who treat sin as quite harmless for the believer. What must we say of people who teach that all believers sin daily "in word, thought and deed," and who even laugh at others who claim there is real deliverance through Christ? For one thing, they may be using an improper definition of sin, including in the same category innocent mistakes with the most willful disobedience.[25]

Beyond an error of definition, there is the dangerous error of belittling the seriousness of sin. This passage from St. John says those who continue sinning are children of the devil. The "modified Calvinists" frequently assure believers they can continue to sin and be entirely safe as children of God. They use more than one interpretation to evade the force of the passage. For one, they adopt a different definition here, making this passage refer to deliberate and habitual sin. But even with the shift in definition, they are not willing to apply the verse to believers. They will not admit that a real believer who lapses into willful, habitual sin is now a child of the devil again.

A second explanation is illustrated by Chafer's comments on the passage:

> The new nature does not commit sin: the old nature can do nothing else. Proof that one is saved is not found in sinless perfection; but is found in the fact that there are new desires and powers in the new creation. These can prevail over the old desires by the power of the Spirit. The Bible simply demands that there shall be some real evidence of the new life from God.[26]

The Bible teaches no such "split personality" as Chafer describes. If this were true, a believer would still be "of the devil" from his old nature, and "of God" by the new nature. The Bible treats whole people—body, soul and spirit (1 Thessalonians 5:23)—not people who belong half to the devil and half to God.

Taylor accents the great danger from such an erroneous doctrine of sin:

> In plain language, the Calvinistic system of predestination, grace, perseverance, and imputed righteousness, means that as a condition of getting to heaven complete deliverance from sin is unnecessary.
>
> Who would say that this does not vitally affect the very foundation of the sin question, and all doctrines relating directly to redemption? Is this a right or wrong conception of sin? If wrong, then the entire Calvinistic system is unscriptural.[27]

Further Scriptural Analysis of Security

Dr. I. Howard Marshall, British scholar and lecturer in New Testament Exegesis at the University of Aberdeen, Scotland, has conducted an intensive investigation into the biblical doctrine of security. The results are presented in his book, *Kept by the Power of God*. His presentation is very objective, and he sets aside a number of the passages which Arminians have claimed as proof for the conditional nature of the believer's security. For example, in the case of Demas, while Marshall believes he was a true disciple who apostatized, he allows that the evidence is not conclusive. After making several such allowances, however, he finds numerous passages which do conclusively support the conditional character of security; that is, the possibility of final loss for a person once saved. A few of them will be given here.

Luke 8:4-15 gives us Jesus' parable of the sower and the four kinds of result. Let us observe the third group in particular: "and that which fell among thorns are they, which, when they have heard, go forth, and are choked with cares and riches and pleasures of this life, and bring no fruit to perfection" (v. 14). Marshall says,

> These appear to be people who receive the Word and make some apparent growth in discipleship, but never reach the stage of producing the fruit which is the evidence of maturity. They yield to worldly temptations and so fall away from whatever faith they had professed.
>
> From this parable, then, we may conclude that the group of disciples will include some who do not persevere in their faith. They lack the ability to withstand testing and temptation. Their faith is real, so far as it goes, but it is overcome by temptation. It lacks the quality of persistence (Luke 8:15).[28]

The first group of hearers did not become believers. "Then cometh the devil, and taketh away the word out of their hearts, lest they should believe and be saved" (v. 12). We should notice here that believing is joined with salvation. We can rightly conclude concerning those on the rock that for awhile they were saved. "These have no root, which for a while believe, and in time of temptation fall away" (v. 13).

One way the unconditional securitists handle this passage is to insist that believing is not genuine unless it overcomes all opposition unto the very end. But such insistence reduces their doctrine of eternal security to a useless truism. The "eternal security of believers" does not then apply to all believers, but only to "true believers" who persevere to the end. The statement "true believers will persevere to the end and be eternally secure" then reduces to the following: "those who persevere to the end will persevere to the end and be eternally secure." There is nothing in that to dispute or debate. But there is nothing in it to encourage new believers, either. They cannot know if they are true believers until they have persevered to the end.

Another way this passage is sometimes treated is to assert that there is no true divine life unless there is fruit. Strombeck writes, for example,

> That which grew among the rocks and the thorns bore no fruit, hence, it had no seed in it, while that which bore fruit did have seed... Thus, the Bible clearly makes the continuing presence of seed a sign of new birth. The absence thereof becomes a sign that regeneration has not taken place.[29]

According to this view, regeneration is not signified by the sprouting of new life from the planted seed, but by the production of fruit when maturity is reached. If this is true, then salvation is by a process of endurance, growth and fruitbearing, and not by receiving and believing the Word of God. Emphatically we declare this is not the teaching of Jesus. He spoke of those who "should believe and be saved," and of those who "for a while believe, and in time of temptation fall away." Salvation comes by believing, not by fruit bearing.

Marshall comments,

> There is no indication that [their faith] is unsound other than the evidence of how the men failed in a crisis... We can conclude only that the character of faith is shown up by testing, and that in this case a lack of steadfastness is evident. But there is no evidence to suggest that it would have been possible to tell in advance that these men would not endure. One might press the details of the parable and argue that the men did not bring forth fruit, which is the evidence of inward character...but this procedure is unwarrantable. To describe the men as hypocrites would be plainly unjustifiable.[30]

The second passage to be examined is Galatians 5:4, "Christ is become of no effect unto you, whosoever of you are justified by the law, ye are fallen from grace." Marshall explains,

> Submission to circumcision indicated a cessation of faith in Christ... It was the expression of an act of repudiation of God's grace manifested in Christ. The person who was circumcized severed himself from Christ and His saving power (Galatians 5:2); he had fallen away from grace.[31]
>
> ...There can be no doubt that in this verse Paul is speaking of the possibility of turning from faith in Christ to an attempt to be justified by the law, and that such an action leads to loss of salvation.[32]

Third, we may look at the multitude of warnings which are given to believers to avoid failure of their faith and the exhortations to abide in Christ. Marshall considers many of them, such as Hebrews 2:1-4; 5:11-6:20; 10:19-39; and 2 John 7-11. For example, here is the exhortation of 1 John 2:28, "And now, little children, abide in him; that, when he shall appear, we may have confidence, and not be ashamed before him at his coming." Marshall summarizes,

> As we noted earlier, these warnings exhort believers not to lose the salvation which they have already received or to surrender the faith which they already profess; they cannot be regarded as commands to believers to test themselves to see if they were truly converted in the beginning. If the Calvinist theory were true, the warnings would necessarily take such forms as: "Make sure that you really were converted," "Beware lest what you think is an experience of salvation by faith is really nothing of the kind," and "Examine yourself to see whether you really are what you profess to be." Naturally some commands of this form are to be found. But the main type of warning is to beware lest one gives up the faith which one already holds or loses the salvation which one already enjoys. Put otherwise, the positive command is not to begin to be a genuine believer but to continue and persevere in the faith which one already has; the believer is not to add some new ingredient to faith, without which it was not true faith, but to maintain the faith. In Johannine terminology, "abiding" is not a fresh quality to be added to faith but the maintenance of a faith already held, and in Hebrews the ideas of perseverance and zeal make the same point. The command is not to go back to the beginning and start afresh with genuine conversion, but to hold fast the faith to the end. The New Testament takes for granted a present experience of salvation of which the believer is conscious. Here and now he may know the experience of Christian joy and certainty. He is not called to question the reality of his experience on the grounds that it may be illusory because he was never truly converted; rather, he is urged to continue to enjoy salvation through abiding in Christ and persevering in faith.[33]

Finally, we consider the *warnings in The Revelation*, which include the following: "But that which ye have already hold fast till I come" (2:25); "He that overcometh, the same shall be clothed in white raiment; and I will not blot out his name out of the book of life, but I will confess his name before my Father, and before his angels" (3:5); "And if any man shall take away from the words of the book of this prophecy, God shall take away his part out of the book of life, and out of the holy city, and from the things which are written in this book" (22:19).

Marshall concludes,

> The emphasis is on faithfulness, witness, and patience through many trials and temptations to the end. It is a life of perseverance, and, if this appears to be a one-sided description which emphasizes the need of human effort, this is because the situation of the Church has led John to emphasize this aspect.
>
> The possibility of failure to endure is mentioned. Christians who fail to persevere will come under judgment (Revelation 2:22f.), and their names will be blotted out of the book of life... There is no reason to suppose that these warnings are purely hypothetical, directed against non-existent dangers; the reverse is the case... Moreover, the reference to the book of life indicates that John is addressing his warning to believers.[34]

To summarize this section: Arminians recognize that while there is abundant assurance concerning the security of the believer, that security is conditioned on faithfulness, a condition which can be met by the aid of the Holy Spirit. This position is attested by a great many passages from God's Word, which must be ignored or badly misinterpreted if a person is still to insist on unconditional security.

Some Cliches of the Security Doctrine

In their efforts to promote this doctrine, the proponents have made popular a number of concise statements. Some of them, such as "once saved, always saved," have already been refuted in the foregoing. It is true only if the condition of faithful perseverance is added.

Another which is similar is "*once a child, always a child,*" or "once a son, always a son." The analogy is given thus by Rice: "When I have become God's child, that is as settled as when I was born my father's child."[35] To show that the analogy is not binding in a spiritual sense, we need only notice that all believers were once children of the devil. If the analogy is binding, they must always remain so. Since children of the devil can become children of God, the analogy is obviously not binding. Jesus said to His hearers one day, "If God were your Father, ye would love me:... Ye are of your father the devil, and the lusts of your father ye will do" (John 8:42, 44). Paul wrote of all believers, including himself, "we all had our conversation in times past in the lusts of our flesh, fulfilling the desires of the flesh and of the mind; and were by nature the children of wrath, even as others" (Ephesians 2:3). Now if it were true that "once a child, always a child," then we would have to conclude that those who were once children of the devil will always be children of the devil; and those who were once children of wrath will always be children of wrath. That would totally prevent any unbeliever from ever becoming a believer and being saved. Such a position is plainly false; it only serves to convince the naive and unthinking.

"*A person who is once born can never be unborn.*" Rice illustrates this position also, when he says, "A child cannot become unborn, and the relationship of a father and child cannot be ended."[36] This also is a subtle way of convincing those who are not careful in their thinking. The Bible never uses the term "unborn," for the opposite of being born is to die, not to be "unborn." The Bible clearly teaches that one who has been born can die. Life does not end by "unbirth," but by death. A fire that is once kindled is never "unkindled," but it can be quenched. A fish that is once caught is never "uncaught," but it can be cast away as worthless. Likewise, a person who is once born can die (both physically and spiritually), and nothing at all is proved by the fact that we do not use the term "unborn" to express the end of life.

"*Eternal life has no end; so a person who has eternal life can never lose that life.*" The force of this argument is removed when we recognize that what is eternal has neither beginning nor ending. If eternal life cannot be lost because it has no ending, then it cannot be gained either, for it has no beginning. Accordingly, a person cannot be saved unless he was eternally saved without a beginning. The answer to this enigma is found in the words of St. John, "And this is the record, that God hath given to us eternal life, and this life is in His Son. He that hat the Son hath life; and he that hath not the Son of God hath not life" (1 John 5:11-12). *Eternal life* is the quality of life which is in Jesus Christ. It has its origin nowhere else. If we receive Him, we have eternal life; if we lose Him, we lose eternal life. It can have both beginning and ending in us—a beginning when we believe on Him for personal salvation; an ending if we cease to believe and follow Him. This need never happen, but it is a possibility which the believer is often urged to avoid.

"*The Bible never speaks of people being resaved or being born a third time.*" The statement is supposed to prove that a person cannot become "unsaved" after once being saved; otherwise the Bible would call him to be saved a second time. Or if the second birth were nullified, the Bible would urge a third birth. Whereas the Bible does not use these precise terms, it does use a number of expressions which denote a return to repeat the first steps of the Christian life. It speaks of renewing, of reviving, of doing the first works again, of being healed from backsliding, and of being renewed again to repentance. The mere use of such phrases does not in itself prove that in each case a person has been totally cut off from God and is being called to restoration; but it does indicate that there is a Bible language concerning the restoration of those who are backslidden, even though it does not involve the terms "third birth" and being "resaved."

True Security

Already we have asserted that Arminians believe in Christian security—even eternal security, if it be understood that it is conditional security. Wesley wrote, "I declare just what I find in the Bible, neither more nor less; namely, that [eternal security] is bought for every child of man, and actually given to every one that believeth. If you call this conditional salvation, God hath declared it so to be..."[37]

Those who defend unconditional security magnify the resources which God provides for the believer, and Arminians do no less. If the former stress God's grace, power, love, mercy, promises and chastening; the Son's substitutionary death, priestly intercession, and indwelling presence; and the Spirit's help in overcoming the world, the flesh and the devil; the latter do likewise. God be praised for the abundant assurance that is given to the believer as encouragement to run the race with patience to the very end!

In particular, it should be pointed out that Arminians do not believe in being saved by works or by self-effort. Chafer says, "To hold over people the superhuman obligation of self-keeping in Christ, is but to encourage them utterly in the purpose of true Christian living and incline them to discount the very standards of God."[38] That is doubtless true, but it is not a charge that applies to orthodox Arminians. If there are people of any theological persuasion that teach security on the basis of self-keeping, they fail to understand the resources that are available to believers. However, there is a personal responsibility involved in perseverance, as Jude shows when he says, "Keep yourselves in the love of God, looking for the mercy of our Lord Jesus Christ unto eternal life... Now unto him that is able to keep you from falling, and to present you faultless before his glory with exceeding joy, to the only wise God our Savior, be glory and majesty, dominion and power, now and ever. Amen" (Jude 21, 24-25). Jude refers here to an element of self-keeping, but he does not thereby extract the joy and assurance from Christian living. He, rather, ends with a burst of high praise, because our self-effort is supported and assured by God's keeping power.

This passage from Jude illustrates what has been our contention from the beginning, that God in His sovereignty has reserved to mankind a limited sphere of personal responsibility concerning his salvation. God provides ample grace and power, but man must respond to it. Even the ability to respond and the strength with which the response is made are gifts of God. But the exercising of the ability and appropriation of divine strength involve the human will. As Paul says, "It is God which worketh in you both to will and to do of his good pleasure" (Philippians 2:13). This does not mean that God wills and does everything in our stead, but that He enables us, by His inworking, to will and do what pleases Him. He enables us to "keep ourselves" in the limited sense indicated by Jude, but this does not mean that we are left totally to our own strength for salvation. Far from it! No person could be saved in such a case. God never asks us to accept a responsibility that He will not enable us to discharge. After one of Paul's strongest exhortations, he appends this assurance: "Faithful is he that calleth you, who also will do it" (1 Thessalonians 5:24). When God calls us to any duty or response, He assures us that His grace is sufficient, if only we will appropriate it in faith and obedience.

It has already been explained that such response of faith is not a work of merit before God. All merit is in Christ, even though it is received by faith that is expressed in obedience.

In contrast to the modified Calvinistic position, Wesleyan-Arminians remember, however, that Christian security is conditional. This does not beget a spirit of fear or insecurity in the heart of the believer if he understand the Bible teaching about how we are kept. If such a spirit arises, it is because of twisted teaching, imperfect understanding, or incomplete obedience which generates unbelief.

Eternal securitists frequently charge Wesleyans with teaching "sinless perfection," meaning either that a Christian can no longer sin, or that if he does sin in even the slightest way, he is cut off from God and must return to be saved all over again. John Wesley chose not to use the term "sinless perfection" because it was so easily misunderstood.[39] He made a distinction, consistent with the Bible, between a single act of sin in contrast to the usual victorious walk of the believer, and the ongoing course of conscious sinning. The first, he held, could be a "sin of surprise,"[40] which might be committed while a believer remained a child of God. The latter is altogether consistent with divine sonship.

St. John has much to say about a believer's assurance as well as warning about the false assurance of the Gnostics and their followers. In 1 John 2:1, he says, "My little children, these things write I unto you, that ye sin not. [The Greek aorist tense indicates a single act of sin.] And if any man sin, we have an advocate with the Father, Jesus Christ the righteous." What it means to have our Advocate with the Father is clarified by reference to 1 John 1:7, "If we walk in the light, as he is in the light, we have fellowship one with another, and the blood of Jesus Christ his Son cleanseth us from all sin." God is not waiting like an eagle-eyed tyrant, ready to cut off instantly any child who slips, stumbles, or commits a sin of surprise. We have an Advocate! If we walk in the light, which means acknowledging what the light reveals and obeying what God says, we always have cleansing and fellowship, and it never terminates. God never cuts people off for ignorance while they are walking in the light they have. It is only when they see in God's clear light what they ought to do and fail to do it—or they fail even to seek God's light—that the cleansing and the fellowship cease.

Quite a different condition is described in 1 John 3:8, "He that committeth sin is of the devil." That refers to one who is going contrary to divine light, in a course of sinning. Such a person is not God's child, whatever he may have been in the past.

God is not eager to cut off any of His children. He seeks to guide and protect every one of them. Those that are weak He wants to strengthen, until they are firmly established. Paul said, "Him that is weak in the faith receive ye, but not to doubtful disputations... Yea he shall be holden up: for God is able to make him stand" (Romans 14:1, 4). Yet even this blessed assurance is balanced with a condition: "And he that doubteth is damned if he eat, because he eateth not of faith: for whatsoever is not of faith is sin" (v. 23).

God's light makes things clear and plain. Paul says, "All things that are reproved are made manifest by the light: for whatsoever doth make manifest is light" (Ephesians 5:13). God shows us what is wrong and what is right. Walking in the light means responding according to what He shows us. If we have been involved in a single sin, walking in the light means confessing it at once and appropriating His forgiveness. As a person refuses to do this, the fellowship is interrupted and the blood ceases to cleanse. Such occurrences of sin will surely be rare, if not entirely absent, as one grows in grace and strength. They are never to be accepted as normal for the Christian life.

St. Paul applied such a disciplined carefulness to his own life. He asserted, "I keep under my body, and bring it into subjection: lest that by any means, when I have preached to others, I myself should be a castaway" (1 Corinthians 9:27). The term castaway, or an equivalent translation from the Greek, is used often in the New Testament, and careful study will reveal that consistently it implies a separation from Christ. Yet Paul was not a morbid doubter about his relation to Christ or his hope of glory. As he faced his last fiery ordeal, forsaken by friends, and spent in body, he uttered his final exultation in victory through Jesus Christ. As we appropriate God's provisions and meet His conditions, we can enjoy the same abounding assurance and join in the same doxology of praise: "The Lord shall deliver me from every evil work, and will preserve me unto his heavenly kingdom: to whom be glory for ever and ever. Amen" (2 Timothy 4:18).

Endnotes

1. *Institutes*, III:xxiv:6.

2. John Calvin, *Institutes of the Christian Religion* (Philadelphia: Presbyterian Board of Publication, 1813), Vol. I, pp. 8-9.

3. *Institutes*, III:ii:11.

4. *Ibid.*

5. Hodge, *Commentary on the Epistle to the Romans*, p. 459.

6. Shank, *Elect in the Son*, p. 214.

7. Shank, *Life in the Son*, p. xix.

8. Shank, *Elect in the Son*, pp. 15, 17.

9. *Ibid.*, p. 16.

10. Roy Hession, *From Shadow to Substance* (Grand Rapids, MI: Zondervan Publishing House, 1977), pp. 169-172.

11. Chafer, *Op. cit.*, p. 105.

12. *Ibid.*, p. 103.

13. Charles C. Ryrie, *A Survey of Bible Doctrine* (Chicago: Moody Press, 1972), p. 133.

14. J. F. Strombeck, *Shall Never Perish* (Chicago: Moody Press, 1966), p. 120.

15. Rice, *Op. cit.*, p. 6.

16. *Ibid.*, p. 8.

17. See John Fletcher, *Works* (Salem, OH: Schmul Publishers, 1974 reprint), Vol. I.

18. John R. Rice, *And God Remembered* (Wheaton, IL: Sword of the Lord Publishers, 1941), p. 34.

19. Hession, *Op. cit.*, p. 154.

20. Wesley, *Works*, X, p. 291.

21. Additional passages linking salvation with faith are John 3:15, 16; 11:25; 12:46; 20:31; Acts 13:39; Romans 9:33; 10:13; etc.

22. I. Howard Marshall, *Kept By the Power of God* (Minneapolis, MN: Bethany Fellowship, Inc., 1969), p. 187.

23. Other passages involving obedience include Matthew 19:17; John 14:21-24; 15:10;

James 1:21-25; etc.

24. Marshall, *Op. cit.*, p. 128.

25. This subject is treated at length in the writer's book, *The Holy Way* (Salem, OH: Schmul Publishers, revised edition, 1981), pp. 151-54.

26. Chafer, *Op. cit.*, p. 102.

27. Taylor, *Op. cit.*, p. 19.

28. Marshall, *Op. cit.*, p. 63.

29. Strombeck, *Op. cit.*, p. 116.

30. Marshall, *Loc. cit.*

31. *Ibid.*, p. 110.

32. *Ibid.*, p. 241.

33. *Ibid.*, pp. 201-202.

34. *Ibid.*, p. 175.

35. Rice, *Ibid.*, p. 17.

36. *Ibid.*

37. Wesley, *Works*, X, p. 254.

38. Chafer, *Op. cit.*, p. 113.

39. Wesley, *Works*, XI, p. 396.

40. *Ibid.*, pp. 93-94.

8

An Analysis of Romans Nine to Eleven

In Chapter 1 it was shown that Arminius, formerly a high Calvinist, was dissuaded from that position by an intensive study of Romans, Chapters 9 to 11. Chapter 3 contains a background study in the predestination passage of Romans 8:29-30. We are now ready to look more closely at those chapters which, although they have often been considered a stronghold for Calvinistic theology, were instrumental in turning Arminius away from that position.

Earlier in his epistle, St. Paul declared the fact that if the Jews did not keep the righteousness of the law, their circumcision would be made uncircumcision (2:25). Furthermore, if the Gentiles should keep the righteousness of the law, their uncircumcision would be counted circumcision (2:26). Then he went a step farther and declared that Gentiles could be justified by faith apart from possession of the law: "But now the righteousness of God without the law is manifested, being witnessed by the law and the prophets; even the righteousness of God which is by faith of Jesus Christ unto all and upon all them that believe: for there is no difference: for all have sinned and come short of the glory of God... Therefore we conclude that a man is justified by faith without the deeds of the law" (3:21-23, 28).

Such teaching was most offensive to the Jewish teachers. They resented the preaching of salvation to Gentiles, especially when they were offered salvation without becoming circumcised and fulfilling all of the Jewish ceremonies. When it was added that Jews could be cut off from God by refusing faith in Jesus Christ, their indignation rose even more. They believed that since the Jews were God's elect people, they were predestined to divine favor. They could not understand how it was possible for them to be set aside while the gospel was preached to the Gentiles. Surely God's predestination meant that they, and they only, were assured of His eternal blessing. How could they ever be bypassed and the Gentiles brought into divine favor? That appeared to them to be a contradiction of God's predestination.

The objection of the Jews can be concisely expressed in this question, which is carefully addressed by the Apostle: "Does not the word of God become of none effect, if those of the Jews who seek righteousness, not of faith, but of the law, are rejected of God?"[1] The treatment of the question by St. Paul can be divided into three section, as follows: 1) God's fairness to Israel in the past, Romans 9:1-29; 2) Human responsibility in the present, 9:30-10:21; and 3) God's purpose for the future, 11:1-36.[2]

God's Fairness to Israel in the Past

When the Jewish leaders were told that by their unbelief of the gospel of Christ they were cut off from God, they had a serious objection. If they were elect through Abraham, then this assertion about the gospel must be false. If this assertion is indeed true, then the election of God—His choice of Israel—has failed. In brief, Paul's claim about the gospel contradicted their understanding of God's sovereign election and predestination of Israel. St. Paul met their objection seriously and convincingly.

Israel's Advantages

The apostle first stressed the advantages of Israel: "the adoption, and the glory, and the covenants, and the giving of the law, and the service of God, and the promises" (v. 4). He expressed deep love for his people and assured them that he would be willing to go to any extreme limit to bring them to Christ and His salvation. He admitted that they were God's adopted people, chosen from among the nations to be particularly His own. The glory and worship of God had been observed among them as among no other people. And the promised Messiah had come in their lineage. They were rich indeed!

The Principle of Selection

Next the writer explained the principle by which God chose His own people (vs. 6 to 13). Was it according to natural descent, so that all of Abraham's descendants were automatically included in the benefits, or were there other principles involved? Immediately he gave the answer, "For they are not all Israel, which are of Israel; neither, because they are the seed of Abraham, are they all children: but in Isaac shall thy seed be called. That is, They which are the children of the flesh, these are not the children of God: but the children of the promise are counted for the seed" (6-8). Not all of the descendants of Abraham were included in the covenant benefits, Ishmael having been rejected and Isaac chosen. So it can already be announced (v. 6) that the Word of God is not nullified if some of Israel are cut off from the benefits of the covenant. God has never been bound to give His benefits just on the basis of biological descent.

In Verse 8 two lines of descent are distinguished: children of the flesh and children of the promise. These are not biological but spiritual classifications. Both Ishmael and Isaac were biological descendants of Abraham, but only Isaac was a child of promise. Ishmael came through Abraham's lapse into fleshly planning apart from faith. So Ishmael represents the "children of the flesh," or children of unbelief. Paul made this distinction very clear in Galatians 4:22-31: "But he who was of the bondwoman was born after the flesh; but he of the freewoman was by promise" (v. 23). Ishmael the firstborn would naturally have been the heir of Abraham, but God was not bound to choose according to natural descent. He chose the son of promise and illustrated at the very beginning that His emphasis would be on faith in His promises.

Having spoken of Isaac and Ishmael, Paul proceeded to introduce the contrast between Jacob and Esau. The Jews might have thought that Ishmael was rejected just because he was born to a slave woman, and therefore they would have missed the application of God's principle of choice to themselves. So Paul spoke of two brothers who were born to the same mother at the same time. With this equality of background, God again made choice, rejecting the usual priority of the firstborn and putting the second son first in His selection.

This choice was not made according to any merit, for neither son had done anything at all when the choice was made. God's purpose in election was not in any way forced; He was perfectly free to act as He would. Yet there was a purpose according to which God acted, as Paul declared: "For the children being not yet born, neither having done any good or evil, that the purpose of God according to election might stand, not of works, but of him that calleth" (9:11). Although at this point Paul did not make that purpose of God explicit, he did in other places, including the conclusion of this chapter: "What shall we say then? That the Gentiles, which followed not after righteousness, have attained to righteousness, even the righteousness which is of faith. But Israel, which followed after the law of righteousness, hath not attained to the law of righteousness. Wherefore? Because they sought it not by faith, but as it were by the works of the law" (9:30-32). *The purpose of God in election is thus the calling of those who believe in Jesus Christ.* Arminius summarized, "They are not embraced in that purpose, who are of the works of the law, but only they who are of the faith of Jesus Christ."[3]

When God chose the younger brother, He said, "The elder shall serve the younger" (v. 12. Compare Genesis 25:23). What was the principle of this selection? Paul has made it plain that God is free to choose as He wills. Nevertheless, He does choose according to principles that He has revealed. We can easily discover the principle manifested in the choice of Jacob, for Paul explains, "As it is written, Jacob have I loved, but Esau have I hated" (v. 13). That sentence "is a Hebrew idiom meaning, 'I have preferred Jacob to Esau.'"[4] It must be observed that this statement was not made by the Lord at the time of the selection of Jacob, but by the prophet Malachi many centuries later (Malachi 1:1-5). There it is explained that two nations rather than merely two individuals are under consideration, for after making the statement the prophet continued by talking of Edom, the nation that came from Esau: "They shall build, but I will throw down; and they shall call them, The Lord hath indignation forever" (v. 4). It is a *people*, and not a single person, that is hated, or rejected, in favor of Jacob and his descendants. The basis of that selection is that the Lord hath indignation against this people forever for their wickedness. Now it has already been shown that God did not make this choice originally because of either good or evil in the twin brothers, for they had done neither when the selection was made. The choice, therefore, must have been made through divine foreknowledge of what they would become. It is this fact which St. Paul presented in Romans 9:12-13.

To summarize thus far: God's choice was not made on the basis of biological heredity. It was made through His own sovereign purpose and according to His foreknowledge of what the two nations would become. Esau's descendants would be a wicked nation, Edom, called "children of the flesh." Israel would become a nation of promise, and from them would arise a people of faith in Christ.

God's Freedom to Select

Beginning with Romans 9:14, St. Paul considered anticipated objections from the Jews. He wrote, "What shall we say then? Is there unrighteousness with God? God forbid." He expected that the Jews would respond to his foregoing arguments by saying that if God rejected one person and chose another without reference to merits, then God was not acting righteously. Paul first denied such an assertion. There cannot possibly be unrighteousness with God. Then he proceeded to show, with illustration from various parts of Scripture, that God was perfectly free to make selection of individuals upon whom He would manifest His mercy—for it is mercy, and not human merit, which is basic in His choices. Mercy cannot be demanded as a duty, for if it were a duty, it would no longer be mercy.

The first example cited is that of Moses, who gave his reasons why God ought, as a duty, to spare the disobedient nation of Israel at Mt. Sinai (Exodus 32:11-13; 33:31-32). Rather than have the nation destroyed, Moses asked that his own name be blotted out before God. The reply was that God would blot out the name of those who sinned (Exodus 32:33). When Moses asked to see God's glory, the request was granted, and God announced the principle, "I will have mercy on whom I will have mercy, and I will have compassion on whom I will have compassion" (Romans 9:15; Exodus 33:19). St. Paul added, "So then it is not of him that willeth... but of God that showeth mercy" (Romans 9:16).

Moses asserted his own will in the matter and appealed to God on the basis of duty. In God's response He showed what duty would require: the blotting out of those who sinned. If He spared Israel, it would be mercy and not duty. Further, if He showed His glory to Moses, that would also be by mercy. Moses was a noble intercessor, and his petition was granted. It was not granted, though, because of the mere assertion of his own will or the appeal to duty, but purely because of mercy.

Calvinists have taken this passage to mean that God considers no other condition than sheer naked sovereignty in displaying His mercy. The Bible amply illustrates otherwise. Many passages show that mercy is granted on condition of repentance and obedience. "He that covereth his sins shall not prosper: but whoso confesseth and forsaketh them shall have mercy" (Proverbs 28:13. See also Exodus 20:5-6; Deuteronomy 7:9-10; Psalm 103:11, 17-18; Isaiah 55:7; and Hosea 10:12-13 as other examples).

A further advance in St. Paul's thought appears in Romans 9:17-18, where the case of Pharaoh is considered. It has been taught by many Calvinists that God created Pharaoh to be reprobated and hardened his heart specifically for the purpose of destroying him. That is not what Paul was teaching, however, when he said, "Therefore hath he mercy on whom he will have mercy, and whom he will he hardeneth" (v. 18). The fact is that God showed great mercy on Pharaoh, and the hardening came through resisting such mercy. The expression "For this same purpose have *I raised thee up*" does not refer back to creation, but rather to the repeated protection of Pharaoh in the midst of the plagues on Egypt, when so many other persons and animals were being destroyed. The fault was with Pharaoh, but he was spared while others were brought to death. God showed mercy and caused him to stand in the midst of the plagues. (The Hebrew expression means "to cause to stand"[5]).

God's purpose was to show His power in Pharaoh. He had shown wonderful mercy to him, and during that time the king was free to yield to God. This fact is revealed in God's word to Pharaoh in Exodus 9:16-17: "And in very deed for this cause have I raised thee up, for to show in thee my power; and that my name may be declared throughout all the earth. As yet exaltest thou thyself against my people, that thou wilt not let them go?" Pharaoh exalted himself, and of his own will refused to let the people go. Since it was a matter of his will, he was held responsible, for he could have done otherwise.

Special attention needs to be given to the thought of hardening the heart. It is repeatedly said that God hardened Pharaoh's heart (Exodus 9:12; 10:1; etc.), and also that Pharaoh hardened his own heart (Exodus 8:15; 9:34; etc.). Obviously, there was an interaction of God's actions and Pharaoh's reactions. The hardening was not a single absolute act of God, but a process that is progressively traced in the biblical record. God gradually intensified the force of plagues upon the land, sparing the king to express his reaction. Step by step in that reaction his resistance grew until he not only withstood God but his own wisest counselors as well (Exodus 10:8-11).

An exhaustive study has been made by Forster and Marston of three Hebrew words for "harden" in the narrative, and the conclusion reached is as follows"

> The Bible does not teach that God made Pharaoh unrepentant. The main word used for hardening of Pharaoh's heart is *chazaq*, and it seems to mean that God emboldened or encouraged Pharaoh's heart so that he had the stubborn courage to stand even in the face of frightening miracles.
>
> The verb *qashah* occurs only twice in the context of the hardening of Pharaoh's heart, and refers to the effects of the whole process of God's dealings and Pharaoh's reactions.
>
> The phrase "made heavy" his heart [*kabed:* Exodus 10:1] is used only once with God as the agent of making heavy. This comes just after Pharaoh himself has rejected his final solemn warning, and has made his own heart heavy. It seems to indicate that God was actively involved in stimulating and allowing the process.
>
> God never prevents anyone from repenting.
>
> "Have I any pleasure in the death of the wicked? says the Lord God: and not rather that he should return from his way and live?"[6]

The work of God was thus performed in full recognition of the king's free will. The latter refused the commands of God and brought judgment upon himself. The One who had shown mercy so often, offering Pharaoh a real chance to escape judgment, had a perfect right to allow those very manifestations of mercy, when resisted, to bring hardness and ripeness for awful judgment.

In summary, a careful study will show that hardening of heart results from a response of unbelief, or a refusal to hear, when God shows His mercy in an invitation to repentance.

We should remember that Paul's teaching was directed to the people of Israel, and the example of Pharaoh was applicable to them as a nation. How often had mercy been manifested only to be refused! Listen to the words of 2 Chronicles 36:14-16, a review of the reason why God allowed that nation to go into Babylonian captivity:

> Moreover all the chief of the priests, and the people, transgressed very much after all the abominations of the heathen; and polluted the house of the Lord which he had hallowed in Jerusalem. And the Lord God of their fathers sent to them by his messengers, rising up betimes, and sending; because he had compassion on his people, and on his dwelling place: but they mocked the messengers of God, and despised his words, and misused his prophets, until the wrath of the Lord arose against his people, till there was no remedy.

In his epistle to the Romans, St. Paul had already stressed the matter of progressive hardening, its causes and its consequences. He said, "Despisest thou the riches of his goodness and forbearance and longsuffering; not knowing that the goodness of God leadeth thee to repentance? But after thy hardness and impenitent heart treasurest up unto thyself wrath against the day of wrath and revelation of the righteous judgment of God; who will render to every man according to his deeds... unto them that are contentious, and do not obey the truth, but obey unrighteousness, indignation and wrath, tribulation and anguish, upon every soul of man that doeth evil, of the Jew first, and also of the Gentiles" (Romans 2:4-9). Pharaoh was a Gentile, and his example was given. But the same principle applied also to the Jews, who had seen even greater displays of mercy than Pharaoh had. Other examples of the causes of hardening can be found in Nehemiah 9:28-29; Jeremiah 19:15; Acts 19:8-9; Mark 16:14; and Hebrews 3:7-13; to mention only a few.

God's Freedom to Use for a Purpose

A new section begins in verse 19, showing that God is free to use people for

His own purpose. "Thou wilt say then unto me, Why doth he yet find fault? For who hath resisted his will?" In this verse, just as in verses 6 and 14, Paul assumed an argument from his opponents. The first concerned the truthfulness of God, the second, His righteousness, and the third, His sovereignty. In their objection, Paul's opponents revealed their idea of predestination. They assumed that the will of God was irresistible and that, if God showed His wrath upon Pharaoh, it was because He had foreordained that Pharaoh should rebel and be brought into divine wrath. Paul's answer is against such a view, which was held by the early Calvinists as well as by the Jewish leaders of Paul's day. The difference is this: those Jews said that if God predestined men to wrath, He should find no fault with the sin in them which merited that wrath. The Calvinists, on the other hand, said that since God had predestined men to sin and wrath, He could justly pour His wrath upon them.[7]

Paul's response was twofold: he first rebuked the attitude revealed in the objection; then he answered that objection. He rebuked it by showing that they were creatures while God is the Creator, and they are not right in condemning God for what He does. We should recognize that in their objection the Jews acknowledged Paul's use of Pharaoh's case as applying to themselves. In effect they were saying, "Since we are God's predestined people and are under His sovereign control, if God has hardened us He should not punish us for that hardness." Numerous commentators understand Paul's meaning thus. Dummelow, for example, commented concerning these verses, "It is now objected that if God's will is irresistible, He ought not to blame the Jews."[8] And Whedon said, "The Jew's question, divested of its petulant words, is this: Since in our downfall, typified thus by Pharaoh's overthrow, God, as you say, has it all his own way, why does he hold us Jews responsible?"[9]

This understanding of the passage shows how improper is the Calvinistic use of these verses. Paul said, "Nay but, O Man, who art thou that repliest against God?" They interpret him as taking the position of a predestinarian and reproving those who object to predestination. The truth is just the opposite: he was reproving the Jews for their strong defense of predestination as applying to themselves.

We may summarize the Jewish position as follows: "Since God in His sovereignty has predestined us as His chosen people, it would not be just for Him to reject us even for hardness of heart; for it is His sovereign power that has brought that very hardness upon us." We have seen Paul's reproof of such a position; now we will see how he answered it.

He used another Old Testament passage in his answer, referring to Jeremiah's story about the potter and the clay, which had to be reshaped into a lesser vessel when the first one was spoiled. Here are Paul's words: "Hath not the potter power over the clay, of the same lump to make one vessel unto honour, and another unto dishonour? What if God, willing to show his wrath, and to make his power known, endured with much longsuffering the vessels of wrath fitted unto destruction: and that he might make known the riches of his glory on the vessels of mercy, which he had afore prepared unto glory..." (vv. 21-23). The parallel passage is found in Jeremiah 18:1-10, where the application to Israel is explicitly made, "O house of Israel, cannot I do with you as with this potter? saith the Lord. Behold, as the clay is in the potter's hand, so are ye in mind hand, O house of Israel" (v. 6).

If there were a perfect parallel between the type and its antitype, there would be merit in the Calvinistic contention that God, simply to display His absolute sovereignty, chooses one person to be reprobated and another to be saved, without reference to the faith or obedience of either. But there is not such a perfect parallel, as the prophet immediately reveals. The clay has no power of volition, to act or react in response to the potter. The fault was in the clay, however, and not in the will of the potter. In Israel's case there is volition involved, and the parallel is between the passive resistance of the clay and the active resistance of Israel to the will of God. The Lord explained His meaning in the parable thus: "At what instant I shall speak concerning a nation, and concerning a kingdom, to pluck up, and to pull down, and to destroy it; if that nation, against whom I have pronounced, turn from their evil, I will repent of the evil that I thought to do unto them. And at what instant I shall speak concerning a nation, and concerning a kingdom, to build and to plant it; if it do evil in my sight, and that it obey not my voice, then I will repent of the good, wherewith I said I would benefit them" (vv. 7-10). Jeremiah proceeded to call Israel to repentance lest calamity should come upon them, they should be scattered, and their land should be left desolate. Unlike the clay, Israel was fully responsible for what was happening to them as a nation, because they had willfully resisted the commands and warnings of God.

There are two pairs of contrasting expressions which, when properly understood, assist in clarifying the meaning of the apostle in this important section. The first is between the two words for "power," in verses 21 and 22.

Verse 21 (quoted above) speaks of the potter's *power* over the clay, to make one vessel to honor and one to dishonor. The word is *exousia*, which means the rightful authority to choose a course of action and to carry it out. The application to Israel is that God has a right to choose some to honor and some to punishment, not whimsically, but on the basis of principles which have already been discussed.

The word for power in verse 22 is *dunaton* (from *dunamai*) and means the ability or strength to do something. In the present context, God's power is shown in His judgment upon the vessels of wrath, just as He showed it in the destruction of Pharaoh. The reasoning is thus: if it is right for God to express mercy to some and wrath to some, according to His own wise principles of conduct, then it is right for Him to express that mercy at length in order that the display of His righteous wrath may be the more impressive.

The second contrast is between the "vessels fitted to destruction" in verse 22 and the "vessels afore prepared unto glory" in verse 23. This is not an arbitrary choice of God whereby His absolute, unconditioned power is displayed. It refers, rather, to the different end results which come to the "vessels of wrath" and the "vessels of mercy." The vessels of wrath are "fitted to destruction," Paul said. The word is from *katartizo* and means to be thoroughly adjusted, prepared, fully qualified, and ripened. This does not refer to what God designed the people for in the beginning, but what *they prepared themselves* for by their persistent disobedience. Take Pharaoh as an example. By his stubborn rebellion, he was *preparing himself* thoroughly for a mighty display of God's wrath upon him. And Israel was doing so likewise, not only be refusing a long line of prophets, but now by refusing their Messiah as well. The "*fitted themselves* to destruction."

The "vessels of mercy," in contrast, were *proetoimaxo, prepared or appointed beforehand.* Concerning this, God's advanced preparation, Dummelow commented,

> St. Paul does not say that God's purpose is to save some and reject others, but "that he might have mercy upon them all," (11:32). In pursuance of this purpose first the Jews, and then Christians, specially Gentile Christians, were called to hold and spread the divine knowledge… On the other hand, he does not say that they could not rebel against God or forsake Him (11:20f).[10]

God has called all people, both Jews and Gentiles, in mercy, and He has made preparations whereby all may share His glory. Those who respond in faith to His call shall know the "riches of his glory." Those who persistently refuse the call may be "endured with much longsuffering," but they are preparing themselves for a mighty display of God's wrath by their refusal.

God's Freedom to Call the Gentiles

Having announced God's "advanced preparation unto glory" (v. 23), Paul proceeded to show that such preparation included Gentiles as well as Jews. His repeated reference to prophetic scriptures in the next section (vv. 24-29) shows that God not only would include obedient Gentiles in His plan, but that He would reject disobedient Jews. God did intend to save the people of Israel, but He expected to use them as witnesses to the Gentiles (Isaiah 42:6; 43:21; 49:6). They failed of that purpose, becoming proud and exclusive in their religious exercises. So God called the Gentiles through the gospel, as Hosea had prophesied (Hosea 2:23 and 1:10). Then He rejected the nation of Israel as a whole, saving only a remnant, as He had prophesied through Isaiah (Isaiah 10:22; 11:11; 1:9).

The Jews in refusing to recognize Gentiles as legitimate parts of the church were actually ignoring or misinterpreting their own prophets. In their prejudice they apparently did not want to discover God's purpose; their pride blinded them to the truth. It appears almost as great a blindness for high Calvinists to assert that there are large segments of humanity which God deliberately chooses to damn rather than to save, when there are so many scriptures that assert His desire for all men to come to repentance and eternal life.

Verse 28 says, "For he will finish the work, and cut it short in righteousness: because a short work will the Lord make upon the earth." This refers to a judgment scene in which a decision is announced. Israel has been judged and found worthy of sentence. The nation was to be set aside while another nation received the benefits of grace. In the meantime, however, any individual of any nation might receive saving grace through faith.

Human Responsibility in the Present

St. Paul moved toward a conclusion concerning God's treatment of Israel. The conclusion is this: God's working takes faith into account. There is human responsibility involved. Predestination is not just an arbitrary display of God's power; it is based on human response to God's call.

In announcing that conclusion, Paul first explained Israel's departure from righteousness, then showed true righteousness comes by faith rather than by the works of the law. The climax of his argument is in his announcement that Israel missed the righteousness of faith, while Gentiles found it through the gospel. This is given at the close of Chapter 9: "The Gentiles, which followed not after righteousness, have attained to righteousness, even the righteousness which is by faith. But Israel, which followed after the law of righteousness, hath not attained to the law of righteousness. Wherefore? Because they sought it not of faith, but as it were by the works of the law" (vv. 30-32). Then he included quotations from Isaiah 8:14 and Isaiah 28:16 to show that the ancient prophet foresaw Israel's rejection of their Messiah—the stumblingstone— through unbelief.

Israel's Departure from Righteousness

In the beginning of Chapter 10, Paul showed how Israel missed true righteousness. First, in their zeal they were ignorant of God's righteousness. Seldom have there been more zealous people, who adhered fiercely to their traditions and persecuted even to death those who would not follow them. Their own Messiah came under their zealous wrath because He did not rigorously conform to their standards. Yet they were ignorant of the truth, not because of lack of information, but because they were not willing to receive the truth. Second, they were self-righteous. They refused to see their own sin but exalted themselves by performing what they considered to be the works of the law. Third, and most important, they refused the righteousness of Christ. The law pointed clearly to Him as the fulfilment of righteousness, but the Jews would not believe in Him, so missed that righteousness which comes by faith.

Righteousness for All by Faith

By quoting from Moses, St. Paul enforced his contention that Jesus is the Messiah foretold in the Old Testament. The Mosaic passage is Deuteronomy 30:12-14, which concludes with these words: "The word is very night unto thee, in thy mouth, and in thy heart, that thou mayest do it." Reference to the context will reveal that the law of God in the heart becomes the basis either for belief unto life or for disobedience unto death. St. Paul applied this to the Word of the gospel which must be received by faith. Then he quoted again from Isaiah 28:26 ("Behold, I lay in Zion for a foundation stone, a tried stone, a precious corner stone, a sure foundation: he that believeth shall not make haste") and applied it directly to Jesus the Messiah. True righteousness, then, even as presented by

Moses, is by faith in Jesus Christ.

In the remainder of the chapter the apostle developed this view of the universality of the gospel message. He made what was for the Jews an astounding statement, since they considered themselves exclusive favorites of God: "There is no difference between the Jew and the Greek: for the same Lord over all is rich unto all that call upon him" (Romans 10:12). The call of God has been given for all men everywhere; He is not partial to any one group to the exclusion of others. In verse 18 Paul asks, "Have they not heard?" and he answers affirmatively by quoting from Psalm 19:4, "Their line is gone out through all the earth, and their words to the end of the world." This plainly includes the Gentile peoples of the world who have the light of nature and conscience even where they are denied the Word of the gospel. God's call is universal; none are left out! The Jewish predestinarians of that day needed to hear that word, just as the Calvinistic predestinarians have needed it in more recent times.

The distinction between the saved and the unsaved is not in the sovereign election of God, but in the response made to His call. Isaiah lamented, "Lord, who hath believed our report?" (quoted in Romans 9:16). There have always been those who choose not to believe even after they receive God's call to salvation.

The chapter closes with two more quotations from Old Testament prophets (there are eleven in this one chapter). In the first, it was foretold that Israel would be provoked to jealousy by Gentile nations (Deuteronomy 32:21); in the second, Israel is called a disobedient and gainsaying people, to whom God had stretched forth His hands all day long.

In summary, Chapter 10 reveals that they would not receive and obey the word of their own Scriptures. It was not from God's arbitrary election that they were left in disbelief, but because of their personal response to the Word that pointed to the Messiah. At the same time, there were those from among the Gentiles who did respond in faith to the gospel call and found what Israel missed.

God's Purpose for the Future

Chapter 11 contains an exultation because of the prospect of Israel's eventual salvation. Chapter 9 began with the cry of a heavily-burdened heart because of Israel's loss. This one ends with a psalm of praise because God in His wisdom has provided for their recovery.

The Rejection of Israel only Partial

The chapter is divided into two parts, each of which begins with a question. First, "Hath God cast away his people?" The meaning is, has God entirely rejected His people? The answer is a strong negative. In proof Paul declared that he was himself a Jew and he was not cast away from God. Moreover, just as there was a remnant of faithful people in Elijah's day, so there is in the present time.

In connection with the remnant, Paul introduced the term "election of grace": "Even so then at this present time also there is a remnant according to the election of grace" (v. 5). It is imperative that we understand the meaning. It refers to that remnant from among the Jews who believed on Jesus as the Messiah. In Romans 4:16 ("Therefore it [justification] is of faith, that it might be by grace") and in Ephesians 2:8 ("For by grace are ye saved through faith"), the connection between grace and faith is clearly established. One cannot be saved by grace without faith. The election of grace is then the election according to faith. Whereas Calvinists have insisted that if faith is necessary to salvation it must be considered a work, Paul shows that the opposite is true. Faith is essential to salvation by grace. It is not a work, but a condition of receiving grace unto salvation. The remnant of grace is the remnant who believed on Jesus.

Responsibility for Blindness

Paul spoke of those who refused their Messiah as being blinded: "(According as it is written, God hath given them the spirit of slumber, eyes that they should not see, and ears that they should not hear;) unto this day" (v. 8). Quoting Psalm 69:23, he continued, "Let their eyes be darkened, that they may not see, and bow down their back alway" (v. 10). From a superficial reading of these passages, it might appear that God was totally responsible for the blindness of Israel. A closer look will reveal otherwise. The first quotation is from Isaiah 29:10. Within the immediate context, we have these statements about Israel: "This people draw near me with their mouth, and with their lips do they honour me, but have removed their heart far from me" (v. 13); "Woe unto them that seek deep to hide their counsel from the Lord" (v. 15); "Surely your turning of things upside down shall be esteemed as the potter's clay" (v. 16). All of these words came from the Lord Himself, and He placed the blame squarely upon Israel for their condition. Because they had removed their own hearts from God, hid their counsel from the Lord, and turned things upside down, God would visit blindness upon them. Jesus spoke a related truth in Matthew 13:14-15 as he explained why He used parables. Quoting from Isaiah 6:9-10, He said of the hard-hearted Jews, "In them is fulfilled the prophecy of Esaias, which saith, By hearing ye shall hear, and shall not understand; and seeing ye shall see, and shall not perceive: for this people's heart is waxed gross, and their ears are dull of hearing, and their eyes they have closed; lest at any time they should see with their heart, and should be converted, and I should heal them." Note well the explanation of Jesus here. He said the people closed their own eyes lest they should see and understand and be healed. He expressly placed the responsibility upon the people themselves and not upon some inscrutable purpose of God to reprobate them.

This specific issue, who is responsible for the blindness of men who reject God's truth, is a dividing point between the Calvinists and the Arminians. Calvin allowed that the hardened and blinded may have an immediate responsibility for their condition, but insisted that God is ultimately responsible. Speaking of Jesus' explanation of His use of parables, Calvin wrote,

> It now remains to see why the Lord acts in the manner in which it is plain that he does. If the answer is given, that it is because men deserve this by their impiety, wickedness, and ingratitude, it is indeed well and truly said; but still… it does not yet appear what the cause of the difference is, why some are turned to obedience, and others remain obdurate… The refusal of the reprobate to obey the word of God when manifested to them, will be properly ascribed to the malice and depravity of their hearts, provided it be at the same time added, that they are adjudged to this depravity, because they are raised up by the just but inscrutable judgment of God, to show forth his glory by their condemnation. In like manner, when it is said of the sons of Eli, that they would not listen to salutary admonitions, "because the Lord would slay them" (1 Samuel 2:25), it is not denied that their stubbornness was the result of their own iniquity; but it is at the same time stated why they were left to their stubbornness, when the Lord might have softened their hearts—namely, because his immutable decree had once for all doomed them to destruction.[11]

We are discussing somewhat here from the study of Romans 11 in order to give a scriptural answer to this question of responsibility. Calvin made God ultimately responsible for hardness and reprobation. Arminians reject such an interpretation emphatically as being unscriptural and unfair to the character of God. With relation to Eli's sons, the *Wesleyan Bible Commentary* remarks,

> It is indefensible to claim that it would have been futile for the sons of Eli to listen to their father because the Lord had determined to destroy them anyway…
>
> Sin brings judgment, but repentance brings deliverance. There is a "hardening of the heart," but it is accomplished not by a sovereign act of God but by the

deliberate act of man in his resistance to God's known will and mercy.[12]

Concerning responsibility for the wickedness of Eli's sons, God Himself gave an explanation, as recorded in 1 Samuel 3:11-14,

> And the Lord said to Samuel, Behold, I will do a thing in Israel, at which both the ears of every one that heareth shall tingle. In that day I will perform against Eli all things which I have spoken concerning his house: when I begin, I will also make an end. For I have told him that I will judge his house forever for the iniquity which he knoweth; because his sons made themselves vile, and he restrained them not. And therefore I have sworn unto the house of Eli, that the iniquity of Eli's house shall not be purged with sacrifice nor offering forever.

Cause and effect relationship is clearly established here: the judgment of God on Eli's house was because his sons made themselves vile, and Eli did not restrain them. The Calvinists would reverse this order and make God's decree the cause, and the human wickedness the effect. In this opinion they are going beyond the Word of God and attributing to God a responsibility which He places on sinful men. God did not make Eli's sons vile; they made themselves vile.

It would be easy to find twenty or thirty examples similar to that of Elis's sons, showing that when men deliberately set themselves to resist light and disobey the revealed will of God, God turns to become an enemy. Some illustrations were given in Chapter 6, but more will be included here to confirm the truth under consideration. Here are Isaiah's words concerning the rebellion of Israel (Isaiah 63:7-10):

> I will mention the lovingkindness of the Lord… In all their affliction he was afflicted, and the angel of his presence saved them: in his love and in his pity he redeemed them; and he bare them, and carried them all the days of old. But they rebelled, and vexed his Holy Spirit; therefore he was turned to be their enemy, and he fought against them.

Notice that after loving them, saving them, redeeming them and carrying them, God turned and became their enemy, *because they rebelled against Him*. This was not the outworking of an arbitrary decree to reprobate certain people, but a response to their rebelling. They were responsible for that rebellion, and they bore the consequences when a loving God was estranged from them.

One more example must suffice, from Isaiah 66:3-4, spoken about rebellious Israel: "Yea, they have chosen their own ways, and their soul delighteth in their abominations. I also will choose their delusions, and will bring their fears upon them; because when I called, none did answer; when I spake, they did not hear:

but they did evil before mine eyes, and chose that in which I delighted not." It would be possible to take the statement about God's choosing delusions, and removing it from its context make it appear as if this was an arbitrary election on God's part. However, the context makes it certain that *God's choice was because of Israel's choice.* The responsibility was in them and not in the inscrutable sovereignty of God.

The Rejection of Israel Only Temporary

The apostle raised one question in verse 1; he introduced a second in verse 11: "I say then, Have they stumbled that they should fall?" The answer, like the former, is negative: "God forbid: but rather through their fall salvation is come unto the Gentiles, for to provoke them to jealousy." The contrast between stumbling and falling is a contrast between what is temporary and what is permanent. Paul gave assurance that Israel as a nation has not been permanently cut off from God. In the remainder of the chapter he expounded this theme, which brought him abounding joy. Israel as a nation shall ultimately come to Christ as their Messiah. The salvation of the Gentiles will eventually provoke Israel to jealousy and they will repent of their awful sin committed in rejecting their Savior.

Using a figure from the cultivation of fruit trees, Paul established the conditions of salvation for both Jews and Gentiles. The usual method of cultivation was to take the branch of a good fruit tree and graft it into a wild root. God, however, grafted the wild branches—believing Gentiles—into the good root, which was the beginning of the nation of Israel in Abraham and the patriarchs. The branches are individuals, whereas the root refers to the corporate nation of Israel in its beginning. "Some of the branches were broken off" (v. 17). This refers to Israel except for the "remnant according to the election of grace." Gentiles were grafted into the same olive tree" from which the unbelieving Jews were cut off. The condition on which Gentile individuals may remain in the tree is faith. The Jews were cut off for unbelief, as is stated in Verse 20: "Because of unbelief, they were broken off, and thou standest by faith." Furthermore, those who are now grafted into the tree will be cut off from it if they do not continue in goodness by faith (v. 22).

Finally St. Paul uses the figure of a prison, in verses 30-32, "For as ye in times past have not believed God, yet have now obtained mercy through their unbelief: even so have these also now not believed, that through your mercy they also may obtain mercy. For God hath concluded them all in unbelief, that he might have mercy upon all." The word "concluded" means to be shut up together or imprisoned. Arndt and Gingrich render it thus: "He has imprisoned them all in disobedience."[13]

We have reached the apostle's conclusion. The people of Israel assumed they were forever secure through God's sovereign predestination, and they have been shown in Paul's masterful treatise the falsity of their assumption. All of them are imprisoned, together with the Gentiles, in unbelief and disobedience. The reason is in order that God may show mercy on all. He has not arbitrarily elected some to receive mercy while others receive wrath, entirely apart from any response they make to God's call to salvation through Christ. Jew and Gentile are both alike, in that they are guilty of disobedience and must come to God through the saving mercy of Christ. By faith any person—Jew or Greek—can be saved; through unbelief any person will be lost.

We may well exult with St. Paul, "O the depth of the riches both of the wisdom and knowledge of God! how unsearchable are his judgments, and his ways past finding out!" (v. 33).

Endnotes

1. Arminius, *Op. cit.*, Vol. III, p. 530.

2. Charles W. Carter, *The Wesleyan Bible Commentary* (Grand Rapids, MI: Wm. B. Eerdmans Publishing Co., 1966), Vol. V, pp. 60-74 (adapted).

3. Arminius, *Op. cit.*, Vol. III, p. 538. The relationship between faith and God's purpose is made explicit again in Ephesians 1:9-13.

4. *Beacon Bible Commentary*, Vol. 8, p. 202.

5. Robert Young, *Analytical Concordance to the Holy Bible* (London: Lutterworth Press, eighth edition, revised, 1939), p. 792.

6. Forster and Marston, *Op. cit.*, pp. 169-70.

7. For documentation of the Jewish position, consult Whedon, *Op. cit.*, Vol. 3, p. 350.

8. J. R. Dummelow, *A Commentary on the Holy Bible* (New York: The Macmillan Co., 1908), p. 879.

9. Whedon, *Op. cit.*, Vol. 3, p. 360.

10. Dummelow, *Op. cit.*, p. 877.

11. Calvin, *Institutes*, III:xxiv:14.

12. *Wesleyan Bible Commentary*, Vol. 1, Part II, p. 145.

13. Arndt and Gingrich, *Op. cit.*, p. 781.

9

Predestination and Holiness

One of the distinctive emphases of Wesleyanism is the doctrine of holiness, sometimes called "entire sanctification" or "Christian perfection." In answer to the question, "What may we reasonably believe to be God's design in raising up the preachers called Methodists?" Wesley answered, "Not to form any new sect; but to reform the nation, particularly The Church; and to spread scriptural holiness over the land."[1]

Arminius acknowledged the reality of holiness in personal experience but did not pursue it as a central element in his teachings. He wrote,

> Sanctification... is a gracious act of God, by which He purifies man who is a sinner, and yet a believer, from the darkness of ignorance; from indwelling sin and from its lusts and desires, and imbues him with the Spirit of knowledge, righteousness, and holiness... [It] consists in... the death of "the old man,"... and in the quickening or enlivening of "the new man."[2]

Wesley clarified and strongly advocated the doctrine in his teaching and labored incessantly to bring the truth into personal experience as well. In doing so he was often misunderstood and misrepresented by those who did not share his concerns for Christian experience that measures up to the standards of the Holy Scriptures. Much of the same misunderstanding prevails today. It is to be hoped that the following analysis may serve to remove some of the misunderstanding and misgiving about biblical holiness.

The High Calvinistic View

A strict Calvinistic system of doctrine cannot consistently emphasize the necessity of holiness in heart and life. Because there is so much about holiness in the Bible, the Calvinists, to be biblical at all, must say something about the doctrine. But they are not able to make proper place for it in genuine Christian experience. Indeed many of them look upon any profession of realized holiness as a form of dangerous heresy. The reasons for this follow from their concepts of God and salvation.

The Obscuring of Personal Responsibility

There is, secondly, the emphasis that holiness arises from election as a matter of divine predetermination. Such an emphasis undermines any personal pursuit of holiness or responsibility therefore. Calvin wrote concerning Ephesians 1:4 ("He hath chosen us in him before the foundation of the world, that we should be holy and without blame before him in love..."),

> In the additional statement that they were elected that they might be holy, the apostle openly refutes the error of those who declare election from prescience [foreknowledge], since he declares that whatever virtue appears in men is the result of election... For he shows that whatever favours God bestows in reference to the spiritual life flow from this one fountain, because God chose whom he would, and before they were born had the grace which he designed to bestow upon them set apart for their use.
>
> ...When it is said that believers are elected that they might be holy, it is at the same time intimated that the holiness which was to be in them has its origin in election.[3]

If, as Calvin says, all virtue results from election, then personal responsibility for pursuing virtue, including holiness, is removed. Wesley took note of this fact and objected strongly to it. He preached thus:

> [The doctrine of predestination] directly tends to destroy that holiness which is the end of all the ordinances of God... The doctrine... has a manifest tendency to destroy holiness in general; for it wholly takes away those first motives to follow after it... the hope of future reward and fear of punishment, the hope of heaven and the fear of hell.[4]

The Denial of Practical Holiness

Calvin's doctrine, in the third place, denies that practical holiness is possible in this life. Referring to 1 Thessalonians 3:13 ("To the end he may establish your hearts unblameable in holiness before God..."), he commented,

> These words were strongly urged by the Celestines of old, in maintaining the perfection of holiness in the present life. To this we deem it sufficient briefly to reply with Augustine, that the goal to which all the pious ought to aspire is, to appear in the presence of God without spot and blemish; but as the course of the present life is at best nothing more than progress, we shall never reach the goal until we have laid aside the body of sin, and been completely united to the Lord.[5]

Calvin's claim that we can never reach unblameable holiness in this present life is of course related to his view of inherited sin or depravity. He asserted that the image of God in mankind, including "purity, righteousness and true holiness," was "vitiated and almost destroyed, nothing remaining but a ruin, confused, mutilated, and tainted with impurity."[6] In its full luster it will be seen again only in heaven, according to his understanding. In a later section he wrote of the depravity of the human will and referred to Romans 7:16, 17 ("If then I do that which I would not, I consent to the law that it is good. Now then it is no more I that do it, but sin that dwelleth in me") as follows,

> No good thing dwells in me, of myself, for in my flesh nothing good can be found. Hence follows the species of excuse, It is not I myself that do evil, but sin that dwelleth in me. This applies to none but the regenerate, who, with the leading powers of the soul, tend towards what is good... Who has this struggle in himself, save those who, regenerated by the Spirit of God, bear about with them the remains of the flesh?[7]

The depravity of sin is thus viewed as being so deep and tenacious that it can never be removed until we enter heaven. The regenerated have the sinful, fleshly life to contend with as long as they live.

At this point the high Calvinists appear to be involved in a serious contradiction. They insist that election and predestination are without regard to foreknowledge of what a person is going to be or do in the future, and are dependent simply on the sovereign purpose of God. Since God has elected His people to holiness, as Calvin allowed in an earlier quotation, how is it that God is prevented by foreknowledge of depravity from perfecting that holiness in this present life? Does not holy character bring more glory to God than sinful character? Was not Adam holy in the beginning, as He came from the creative hand of God? Did his fall then thwart God's purpose to have holy character in His creatures? And does God not intend to renew His creation in the image of God, which is righteousness and true holiness? Is then God's purpose in election—unto holiness—thwarted by a condition of depravity which he foreknew should exist in sinful men? How can this be if His election is prior to His foreknowledge? There is surely a contradiction in such reasoning.

Confusion about Responsibility

We may assert, fourthly, that Calvin's teaching is confused regarding a believer's responsibility for pursuing holiness. At one time he spoke as if all responsibility pertains to God alone:

> Paul... thus addresses believers, "Work out your own salvation with fear and trembling. For it is God which worketh in you both to will and to do of his good pleasure" (Philippians 2:12, 13). He ascribes to them a part in acting that they

> may not indulge in carnal sloth, but by enjoining fear and trembling, he humbles them so as to keep them in remembrance, that the very thing which they are ordered to do is the proper work of God—distinctly intimating, that believers act (if I may so speak) *passively*... [italics his].[8]

If believers act *passively*, it can only mean that when they seem to be acting, it is God who in reality is acting upon them, and that in an irresistible way. If they are personally motivated, all the motivation comes from God; if they are not, it is because He withholds the motivation. Any impression of personal responsibility in such a case is merely an impression and can have no basis in fact. Calvin, however, did not leave the matter there. He could not read his Bible without recognizing that in multitudes of instances God assigns personal responsibility to His creatures and holds them accountable for their actions. So in other places Calvin emphasized personal responsibility for holiness. He said,

> If the Lord adopts us for his sons on the condition that our life be a representation of Christ, the bond of our adoption—then, unless we dedicate and devote ourselves to righteousness, we not only, with the utmost perfidy, revolt from our Creator, but also adjure the Savior himself.
>
> ...Let us set evangelical perfection before our eye as the end at which we ought constantly to aim. Let it be regarded as the goal towards which we are to run. For you cannot divide the matter with God, undertaking part of what his word enjoins, and omitting part at pleasure. For, in the first place, God uniformly recommends integrity as the principal part of his worship, meaning by integrity real singleness of mind, devoid of gloss and fiction, and to this is opposed a double mind; as if it had been said that the spiritual commencement of a good life is when the internal affections are sincerely devoted to God, in the cultivation of holiness and justice.[9]

In these passages Calvin came very close to a Wesleyan position, for he made a *condition of our adoption* the representation of Christ in our lives. Unless we are devoted to righteousness, we revolt from our Creator. He is close to Wesley also in defining evangelical perfection as real singleness of mind, internal affections sincerely devoted to God and the cultivation of holiness and justice. He at once disavowed the possibility of our reaching the goal, however, for he immediately continued,

> But seeing that, in this earthly prison of the body, no man is supplied with strength sufficient to hasten in his course with due alacrity, while the greater number are so oppressed with weakness, that hesitating, and halting, and even crawling on the ground, they make little progress, let every one of us go as far as his humble ability enables him, and prosecute the journey once begun. No one will travel so badly as not daily to make some degree of progress... If during the whole course of our life we seek and follow, we shall at length attain it, when

relieved from the infirmity of flesh we are admitted to full fellowship with God.[10]

Again we question Calvin's position. How can it be that the sovereign God, against Whose power no force can be effectively exerted, leaves His creatures longing for holiness, but "so oppressed with weakness, that hesitating, and halting, and even crawling on the ground, they make progress?" If He elects us to holiness, does He allow sin so to thwart His purpose, that His own creatures have too little strength from above to overcome its power? Where is consistency in such a view?

The Mild Calvinistic View

By making more of a place for human will to operate freely, some of the new Calvinists allow the holiness of God to shine forth more clearly. Since God in their view does not reprobate men simply by His sovereign choice, there is no longer need to keep a veil over His holy character. At this point, many mild Calvinists have come to agreement with the Arminian position.

Standing versus State

But while the holiness of God is brought into brighter focus, holiness in believers is removed ever farther from both possibility and necessity. The device which accomplishes this is the separation of "standing" and "state" in the believer's life. In early Nineteenth Century England, the Plymouth Brethren adopted something of Calvinism but minimized emphasis on unconditional election and the decrees of God. They took the "satisfaction theory" of the atonement and from it taught that when Christ died for us, He actually had the believers' sins—past, present and future—imputed to Him, while His perfect righteousness and holiness were imputed to the believer. Faith is acceptance of the "fact" that this has been done once and for all time. The believer thus "stands" before God in the Person of Christ. While in his actual "state" he is still as sinful as ever, God sees him as righteous and holy, because Christ's obedience and purity are substituted for his own. Sin is not put away from the believer, but the robe of Christ's righteousness is put over him, so that God no longer sees him as he is.

Two Natures in Conflict

A further belief is that the believer always has two natures in conflict. At regeneration the new life of Christ is brought within the believer. Yet the old nature of sinful flesh remains and will remain until death. At any time the believer *himself* may decide which nature he will obey, the new or the old. If he follows the direction of the Spirit, he will yield to the new nature. If he does not, the old nature will assert itself. But while such "works of the flesh" may cause an interruption of fellowship with God, they can never bring an end to our relationship with God. They may cause a loss of reward, but never a loss of eternal life.

A multitude of recent writers could be quoted to illustrate these positions, which have been widely adopted from the Plymouth Brethren. The following example is from explanatory notes of the *Scofield Reference Bible*, concerning Romans 7:7 ("For that which I do I allow not: for what I would, that do I not; but what I hate, that do I.")

> The apostle personifies the strife of the two natures in the believer, the old or Adamic nature, and the divine nature received through the new birth... The "I" which is Saul of Tarsus, and the "I" which is Paul the apostle are at strife, and "Paul" is in defeat. In Chapter 8, this strife is effectually taken upon the believer's behalf by the Holy Spirit (8:2; Galatians 5:16, 17) and Paul is victorious.[11]

It is obvious that, in the above scheme, inwrought holiness is neither necessary nor possible. While there are many people holding this view who do indeed thirst after inner purity, their theological interpretation gives them no promise of satisfaction. There is no benefit in having such a thirst, but rather only frustration and defeat, since real cleansing from sin is viewed as impossible.

The Wesleyan Position

Arminius, as we have observed, acknowledged the possibility of real inward holiness wrought by the power of God, but he did not elaborate the doctrine. It remained for Wesley and those who labored with him to amplify it in line with the rich, scriptural teaching on the subject.

The Objectives of Predestination

We observe, first, that predestination has holiness as its objective. There is a proper distinction between election and predestination, as Shank observed:

> Calvin's theological heirs have followed in his footsteps in confusing predestination with election. The two, while closely related and mutually involved, are not the same. Both election and predestination are acts of determination, but the election is God's choice of men *per se*, whereas the predestination looks beyond the fact of the election itself to the *purposes and objectives* comprehended in election...

> Predestination is God's predetermination of the eternal *circumstances* of election: sonship and inheritance as joint-heirs with Christ (Ephesians 1:5, 11) and glorification together with Christ in full conformity to His image (Romans 8:28-30). In Ephesians 1:3-14, the *election* is in view in verse 4 ("he has chosen us in him before the foundation of the world") and the *predestination* is not to election and salvation, but to the *circumstances* of election: adoption as the children of God (v. 5) and participation in an eternal inheritance (v. 11).[12]

Election is then unto certain purposes, and it is well to observe that never in the Scriptures is it said to be either to eternal life or to eternal death. A number of purposes are stated, some of which are mentioned in the foregoing paragraphs from Shank. It is specifically stated in Ephesians 1:4 that God has chosen us to be holy. And, like the other purposes of election, this is by faith in Christ.

Another definitive passage concerning predestination, Romans 8:28-29, includes holiness—conformity to the image of Christ—as one of the purposes.[13] It is true that conformity to Christ is not complete in this life; it involves final glorification, as St. Paul makes clear. Nevertheless, the entire process by which we are brought from our sinful state to glory involves deliverance from sin and full harmony with the will of God. The calling of God is mentioned in Romans, Chapter 1. Justification is treated in Chapters 3 to 5. Full deliverance from sin is proclaimed in Chapters 5 to 8. Then glorification is presented in Chapter 8, beginning with Verse 17. So when St. Paul wrote of the stages by which we are predestined to come to glorification—"Whom he did predestinate, them he also called: and whom he called, them he also justified: and whom he justified, them he also glorified"—he did not mean to exclude deliverance from sin. Indeed, he gave more space to that theme in his masterful treatise than to any of the others.

Conformity to Christ, then, is brought about by stages, and one of those stages is full deliverance from sin, which is provided for us through Jesus Christ. St. Paul made this fact explicit in other places. He wrote the epistles of Colossians and Ephesians at about the same time and included similar themes in both. In Colossians 3:8-14 he wrote, "Put off all these; anger, wrath, malice, blasphemy, filthy communication out of your mouth. Lie not one to another, seeing that ye have put off the old man with his deeds; and have put on the new man, which is renewed in knowledge after the image of him that created him:... And above all these things put on charity, which is the bond of perfectness." The new creation is to be wrought in the image of God, the same theme as Romans 8:29, and that involves a form of Christian perfection, as verse 14 reveals. Ephesians 4:24 is a parallel passage. Referring to the same theme, Paul said, "Put on the new man, which after God is created in righteousness and true holiness." This, combined with the former passage, verifies that the image of God includes righteousness and true holiness; and it is this image in which the new man is created. Should any believe that this involves merely a "standing" before God, rather than an actual change in the believer's "state," observe the Apostle's assertion in 2 Corinthians 3:18: "But we all, with open face beholding as in a glass the glory of the Lord, are changed into the same image from glory to glory, even as by the Spirit of the Lord." The image of Christ's glory is not just a covering draped over our innate sinfulness; we are actually being changed into that image from one state of glory to another, until it is fulfilled in His eternal presence.

Another passage on election is 1 Peter 1:2, "Elect according to the foreknowledge of God the Father, through sanctification of the Spirit, unto obedience and sprinkling of the blood of Jesus Christ…" Again election is not stated to be to eternal life, but unto obedience and sprinkling of the blood of Jesus; and it is through "sanctification of the Spirit." This term as used in the New Testament involves not only setting apart for sacred use, but cleansing from sin as well, Matthew Henry, though writing from a Calvinistic viewpoint, asserted the essential meaning of sanctification as involving inwrought holiness. On the above verse he wrote,

> Every elect person must be sanctified by the Spirit, and justified by the blood of Jesus. God's decree for man's salvation always operates through sanctification of the Spirit and sprinkling of the blood of Jesus. By sanctification here understand, not a federal sanctification only, but a real one, begun in regeneration, whereby we are renewed after the image of God and made new creatures, and carried on in the daily exercise of holiness…[14]

Through this sanctification of the Spirit, the believer is enabled to live in obedience before God, as Peter asserted. There is no suggestion here that Jesus has done all the obeying in our behalf, and that we are thus exempted from the requirement of obedience.

To summarize, the believer is predestined unto holiness; and this in turn involves sprinkling of the blood of Jesus, obedience to His will and conformity to His image.

Christian Victory by the Spirit

Another outstanding distinctive of Wesleyanism is the dynamic provided by the Holy Spirit for Christian life and victory. Calvin declared that the Spirit's primary function in the life of a believer is to bestow faith and assurance.[15]

Wesley in contrast understood that the Spirit in His indwelling presence and power enables the believer to fulfill the law of God and thus to overcome sin daily. He said, concerning those who walk in the Spirit (Romans 8:1),

> They are not condemned... for any present sins, for now transgressing the commandments of God. For they do not transgress them: They do not "walk after the flesh, but after the Spirit." This is continual proof of their "love of God, that they keep his commandments."... Now it is evident, he is not condemned for the sins which he doth not commit at all. They, therefore, who are thus "led by the Spirit, are not under the law:" (Galatians 5:18). Not under the curse or condemnation of it, for it condemns none but those who break it.[16]

Romans 8 is a glowing declaration of blessings available to the believer through the operation of the Holy Spirit. Verse 1 reveals deliverance from condemnation: "There is therefore now no condemnation to them which are in Christ Jesus, who walk not after the flesh, but after the Spirit." This freedom does not pertain to an abstract "standing" before God, but to the way we walk as believers by the help of the Spirit. Condemnation is produced by sin, and freedom from condemnation means freedom from any consciousness of sin (Hebrews 10:1-2).

Verse 2 presents freedom from the control of sin, for the word "law" here refers to a rule or standard operating in the life: "For the law of the Spirit of life in Christ Jesus hath made me free from the law of sin and death." Like a jet rocket which launches astronauts into orbit where they are no longer conscious of the pull of gravity, so the power of the Spirit operating in the believer's life lifts him to a level of victory over sin.

Verse 4 declares that there is a fulfillment of the righteousness of the law within the life of those who walk after the Spirit and not after the flesh. This directly contradicts the notion that Christian righteousness is a mere "standing" before God. It is, rather, an inward "state" produced by the Spirit in which from the heart the believer is fulfilling the law. We can fairly declare that what Christ provided *for us* through His sacrifice, the Spirit purposes to apply *within us* as we walk obediently after His direction.

Verse 9 asserts that when the Spirit of God dwells in us we are no longer "in the flesh." This does not mean, surely, that we are out of the body. Rather, the body is no longer the real sphere of our existence, so that we are controlled by its appeal and appetites. Just as the space men are "not under the law of gravity," even though gravity is still operative all around them, so those "in the Spirit" are not living "in the flesh" and under its rule, even though sin is a very real fact all around them.

The Spirit enables us to "mortify the deeds of the body," as verse 13 says. "Mortify" means to put to death. The word is in the present tense, indicating that a continuous process is involved. In order to avoid sin, the believer must ever deny the desire and actions of the body when they are contrary to God's will. *If we do this*, we shall live. (Notice the repeated conditions to be met if we are to maintain our victory by the Spirit, in vs. 14, 17, etc.).

We have guidance by the Spirit, as shown by verse 14. It is an evidence that we are indeed God's sons, when we are so guided. Further, we have assurance of sonship, the Spirit adding His witness to our own that we are children of God.

Verse 26 indicates that the Spirit "helpeth our infirmities." "Helpeth" is a rich word, meaning literally to stand over against, and to take hold of together with. With reference to our infirmities, seen as a heavy load to be borne, the Spirit stands on the opposite side and lifts with us, carrying all the load which we are not able to bear ourselves! How gracious is His help!

Even though we have the "firstfruits of the Spirit" (v. 23), there is a groaning because of corruption from which we have not as yet been delivered. This is a corruption shared by the whole creation, and though not sinful, it is nevertheless burdensome. It involves the infirmities of which we have spoken, as well as suffering, affliction, tribulation, distress, poverty and such like.

St. Paul indicates that, while our security is conditioned on our willingness to suffer with Christ and to be guided by the Spirit, there is, nevertheless, abundant assurance of our ultimate victory in Him. His final section of Chapter 8 is a song of triumph, in which he magnifies the resources available to bring us to the final glory. It is not just idle theory, either, for St. Paul had found it effective in his own life. Among the "all things" which may be against us, he considers people, circumstances, death, devils, time and space. From people there may come tribulation, distress, persecution or the sword; from circumstances, famine, nakedness, peril, life and death. Among the spirit beings, there are angels, principalities and powers. Time includes things present and things to come; space involves both height and depth. Can any of these things separate us from the love of God.

Out of his own experience, as well as from his profound faith, Paul gave a ready answer. He had been tested by these various forces himself. He could say, "Even unto this present hour we both hunger, and thirst, and are naked, and are buffeted, and have no certain dwelling place; and labor, working with our hands: being reviled, we bless; being persecuted, we suffer it: being defamed, we intreat: we are made as the filth of the world, and are the offscouring of all things unto this day" (1 Corinthians 4:11-13). Again he said, "I know both how to be abased, and I know how to abound: everywhere and in all things I am instructed both to be full and to be hungry, both to abound and to suffer need. I can do all things through Christ which strengtheneth me" (Philippians 4:12-13). He knew the devices of Satan: temptation, discouragement, accusation and fear. In testings and tribulations he did not take second place to any man but was "in labors more abundant, in stripes above measure, in prisons more frequent, in deaths oft. Of the Jews five times received I forty stripes save one. Thrice was I beaten with rods, once was I stoned, thrice I suffered shipwreck, a night and a day I have been in the deep; in journeyings often, in perils of waters, in perils of robbers, in perils by mine own countrymen, in perils by the heathen, in perils in the city, in perils in the wilderness, in perils in the sea, in perils among false brethren; in weariness and painfulness, in watchings often, in hunger and thirst, in fastings often, in cold and nakedness…" (2 Corinthians 4-23-27). That is enough. He had gone through the gamut of sore testings and could exult with mighty conviction, "in all these things we are more than conquerors through him that loved us."

A conqueror has resources more than his enemies. The "all things" of God (Romans 8:32) are more than the "all things" against us (v. 37). It is good to be a conqueror; it is better to be "more than conqueror;" and this we are "through him that loved us." This means we not only have more resources than the enemy, but in addition, we seize his weapons and convert them to our own use, so that we are now richer and not poorer—stronger and not weaker. Just this is what St. Paul assures us of when he says, "We know that all things [there again we see "all things"] work together for good to them that love God, to them who are the called according to his purpose" (v. 28).

The conditional nature of our security is evident even in this encouraging verse. The verbs are in present tense. The sense is that God continues to make all things work to our advantage as we continue loving Him and following the purpose for which He has called us, even conformity to the image of His Son.

The thesis of our present chapter is that predestination is unto a specific purpose, that we should be conformed to Christ. The purpose will be fulfilled when we are glorified, but it includes conformity to His moral image, in "righteousness and true holiness" in this present life by the aid of the Holy Spirit. With this thesis St. John is in perfect agreement when he says, "We know that when he shall appear, we shall be like him; for we shall see him as he is. And every man that hath this hope in him purifieth himself, even as he is pure" (1 John 3:2-3). The constitutional likeness—bodily perfection—awaits our glorification; but the moral likeness—purity of heart and life—is available now through grace. So he can say, "Herein is our love made perfect, that we may have boldness in the day of judgment: because as he is, so are we in this world" (4:17).

Standing and State

According to the Wesleyan understanding, the Scriptures do not support the notion that our Christian standing is something altogether different from our state. The above verse speaks of what we really are: as He is, so are we in this world. Numerous other passages could be brought forth in evidence, of which a few are cited here: "He that saith, I know him, and keepeth not his commandments, is a liar; and the truth is not in him… He that saith he abideth in him ought himself also so to walk, even as he walked" (1 John 2:4, 6); "Whosoever abideth in him sinneth not: whosoever sinneth hath not seen him, neither known him. Little children, let no man deceive you: he that doeth righteousness is righteous, even as he is righteous [the state proves the standing]. He that committeth sin is of the devil" [a sinful state proves that there is no righteous standing before God] (1 John 3:6-8). "Beloved, follow not that which is evil, but that which is good. He that doeth good is of God: but he that doeth evil hath not seen God" [there is no place here for a person who is doing evil, yet is of God, whose standing is righteous while his state is sinful] (3 John 11). One more example may be given, Romans 5:19, "For as by one man's disobedience many were made sinners, so by the obedience of one shall many be made righteous." The reference is to what Christ provides for us in this life, as Calvin admitted. He commented on the verse as follows:

> The meaning is—as by the sin of Adam we were alienated from God and doomed to destruction, so by the obedience of Christ we are restored to his favor as if we were righteous. The future tense of the verb does not exclude present righteousness, as is apparent from the context.[17]

St. Paul is speaking of more than a mere "as if" righteousness, however. The word "made," twice used in the verse, means "to be constituted," and involves a true state or condition. No Calvinist will object to this meaning when it refers to what we became through Adam: sinners, depraved through and through. Wesleyans agree; we were actually constituted sinful by birth because ofAdam's fall. To be consistent, we must put the same meaning into the word when it refers to Christ's work of restoration. He actually makes His people righteous, jut as truly as Adam made them sinful. This cannot allow a mere standing of righteousness while our state remains as sinful as before.

God designs not only to place us *in Christ,* but to make us *like Him* as well. Dr. John Knight, speaking as president of the Wesleyan Theological Society, put it aptly: "To be Christian is to be like Christ. To be like Christ is to be holy. Therefore to be 'Christian' is to be holy. To be becoming increasingly 'Christian' is to be becoming increasingly like Christ, and increasingly holy. In short, Christ-likeness is holiness, and increasing Christ-likeness is increasing holiness."[18] That is the beautiful purpose of predestination.

The Notion of Two Natures

Wesleyanism, finally, does not accept the teaching that our highest state of grace still leaves us with two conflicting natures in perpetual warfare. The sanctifying work of God by His Spirit makes us whole and harmonizes our personalities, not only with God but within ourselves as well. St. Paul surely taught this inner wholeness and harmony when he said, "The very God of peace sanctify you wholly; and I pray God your whole spirit and soul and body be preserved blameless unto the coming of our Lord Jesus Christ. Faithful is he that calleth you, who also will do it" (1 Thessalonians 5:23-24). It is true that the believer, before appropriating the entire sanctification of which Paul speaks, may experience an inner conflict such as is described in Galatians 5:17, "For the flesh lusteth against the Spirit, and the Spirit against the flesh: and these are contrary the one to the other: so that ye cannot do the things that ye would." Two serious errors are involved in the "two-natures" teaching from this verse. First, St. Paul wrote to the Galatian believers as carnal Christians in danger of departing from Christ. They were neither mature nor ideal Christians. Paul did not include himself when he said, "*Ye* cannot do the things that *ye* would." His personal testimony was much better than that, one in which Christ lived in him victoriously. Second is an error in translation, explained by Steele,

> There is no "cannot" in the original: "The flesh lusteth against the Spirit, and the Spirit against the flesh, in order that ye may not do the things that ye would."
>
> The doctrine taught by Paul is that in the regenerate, but not in the entirely

> sanctified, there is a struggle going on, the purpose of which is this: When ye would do the works of the flesh, the Spirit strives to prevent you, and when ye would follow the leading in the Spirit, the flesh opposes. This warfare ceases when "the flesh is crucified," (verse 24) and "the body of sin is destroyed." — Romans 6:6.[19]

Romans, Chapter 7, was taken by Calvin as describing the regenerated life. Most Wesleyans will not allow this, but take its warfare as portraying Paul's efforts to achieve perfection under the law. It includes no inner help from the Spirit and no awareness of victory through Christ, but only self effort under the law, and constant failure. It stands in startling contrast to the assurance and victory of Chapter 8, where the Spirit of Christ delivers from the power of sin within us. Brockett has expressed a Wesleyan position about Romans 7:

> There is… a distinction between the conflict of Romans 7 and Galatians 5:17… In Romans 7:14-24, the Holy Spirit is not mentioned at all; in Galatians 5:17, the conflict is specifically against the Spirit. In Romans 7…we have one who is "quickened by the Spirit of God but seeking holiness in himself, and is *still under law* as a means of promoting piety"… In other words, we have a soul, not "under grace," but "under law," seeking holiness *apart* from the Spirit.[20]

Romans 7 is not an appropriate basis for study of two natures in the believer.

Conclusion

In conclusion, predestination is unto holiness, and that involves a life cleansed and preserved from sin. We have shown St. Paul's song of assurance, given in Romans, Chapter 8. It is most significant that in the array of enemies which he describes as being against us, he does not include sin, either in action or in nature. We have included his testimony of battles which he personally encountered, showing that he knew full well what he was talking about. We now add his testimony of victory over sin, given in 1 Thessalonians 2:10. He says in that chapter that he came to the Thessalonians after shameful treatment at Philippi. The record of Acts 17:1-9 informs us that he had to leave Thessalonica because of mob violence. So he was a man under extreme pressure, enduring hatred, persecution and threat of death. Though in the midst of adversities, here is his testimony: "Ye are witnesses, and God also, how holily and justly and unblameably we behaved ourselves among you that believe." This is not a statement of how God merely saw the righteousness of Christ imputed to him. God saw *him* and witnessed that he was living and acting blamelessly. But his boasting was not in himself; it was in Christ. To the Galatians he said, "I am crucified with Christ: nevertheless I live; yet not I, but Christ liveth in me: and the life which I now live in the flesh I live by the faith of the Son of God, who loved me, and gave himself for faith of the Son of God, who loved me, and gave himself for me" (Galatians 2:20). It was not Christ's life lived *in his stead* and seen of God as covering his sinfulness, but Christ's life lived in St. Paul's body, in this present world. It is nothing less than this to which God has called us, and for which He has predestined us by His grace.

At the end of Romans 7 Paul asked the question, "Who can separate us from sin?" And the answer is, "Only Christ." At the close of Chapter 8, he asked, "Who can separate us from Christ?" And in effect, the answer is, "Only sin." But with the mighty help God affords us, that is not a frightening and unsettling possibility. If we walk in the Spirit, willing to suffer for Jesus' sake, the Spirit makes us constant overcomers and turns each adversity into a blessing. We are predestined unto victory, through faith in Jesus Christ, in spite of the world, the flesh and the devil! Hallelujah!

Endnotes

1. Wesley, *Works*, VIII, p. 299.
2. Arminius, O*p. cit.*,Vol. II, p. 120.
3. *Institutes*, III:xxii:2, 3.
4. Wesley, *Works*, VII, p. 376.
5. *Institutes*, III:xvii:15.
6. *Ibid.*, I:xiv:4.
7. *Ibid.*, II:ii:27.
8. *Ibid.* II:v:11.
9. *Ibid.*, III:vi:3, 5.
10. *Ibid.*
11. C. I. Scofield, *Scofield Reference Bible* (New York: Oxford University Press, 1909), p. 1200.
12. Shank, *Op. cit.*, p. 156.
13. The writer's book *Conformed to Christ* (Cincinnati, OH: Revivalist Press, 1962), enlarges this theme.
14. Matthew Henry, *Commentary on the Whole Bible* (New York: Fleming H. Revell Co., 1935), Vol. VI, p. 1003.
15. *Institutes*, III:i:4.
16. *Works*, V, pp. 90-91.
17. *Ibid.*, II:xvii:3.
18. John A. Knight, "The Supreme Pursuit" (*Wesleyan Theological Journal*, Spring, 1980), p. 9.
19. Daniel Steele, *Half Hours with St. Paul* (Rochester, PA: H. E. Schmul, 1959 reprint), pp. 68-69.
20. Henry E. Brockett, *Scriptural Freedom Sin* (Kansas City, MO: Beacon Hill Press, 1941), p. 137.

Index

J

K

L

M

N

O

P

R

Index of Scripture Passages

If you enjoyed *Creeds in Contrast* by Dale M. Yocum, you will want these other titles by the same author:

•Fruit Unto Holiness/Yocum #2577

A careful study of Romans 6, 7, 8 and 9. Conservative, scriptural and true to the Wesleyan-Arminian position.

•With Peter by the Sea/Yocum #3735

Delves into the books of First and Second Peter to bring the new insights for which this author is so well known. Peter makes reference to Old Testament events, and Yocum illuminates these with a call to holy living.

•This Present World/Yocum #1945

Revised and enlarged. Three very important chapters have been added. A most practical book clarifying the Christians relation to the world—in it, but not of it.

•Armies of God/Yocum #2232

Dr. Yocum was a retired Air Force colonel. This book applies military principles and draws on Biblical battles for applications in spiritual victory today.

CPSIA information can be obtained
at www.ICGtesting.com
Printed in the USA
FFOW03n1619290418
46409297-48191FF

9 780880 191838